Hans L.M. Dassen

A new philosophy of man & humanism

Basic principles

Experience and man as absolute entity
power, religion and politics
individual, society and state
freedom and democracy
environment and the search for meaning

Aspekt Publishers

For all children all over the world,
starting with Hans, Hugo, Sofia, Noor, Max and Nina...

A new philosophy of man & humanism

Anthroopos Foundation Amsterdam
www.anthroopos.com
 | Amersfoortsestraat 27, 3769 AD, Soesterberg | info@uitgeverijaspekt.nl
www.uitgeverijaspekt.nl

Text & Advice – Paul van 't Veld
Helpmeet – Christine Lankwarden
Photography & Image Processing – Tom Feenstra
Design & Layout – Marette Buist
Translation – Carol Stennes

ISBN: 9789464629095
NUR: 130

No problem can be solved from the same level of consciousness that created it.
We must learn to see the world anew.

Albert Einstein

TABLE OF CONTENTS

I Dialogues

1 Reason and religion of the human being Joseph Ratzinger

A search for the essence and the basic questions of human existence
From a dialogue between Jürgen Habermas and Joseph Ratzinger in 2004 on the foundations of the democratic constitutional state (32)

"It is the responsibility of philosophy to accompany critically the development of the individual academic disciplines, shedding a critical light on premature conclusions and apparent 'certainties' about what man is, whence he comes, and what the goal of his existence is. To make the same point in different words: philosophy must sift the non-scientific element out of the scientific results with which it is often entangled, thus keeping open our awareness of the totality and of the broader dimensions of the reality of human existence – for science can never show us more than partial aspects of this existence", in the words of Dr. Joseph A. Ratzinger, former professor of theology, for many years Prefect of the Congregation for the Doctrine of the Faith and, as Pope Benedict XVI, Head of the Roman Catholic Church since April 2005.

He does not "...propose to try ... to define the essence of 'power' as such" and ascertains that "... the rational or ethical or religious formula that would embrace the whole world and unite all persons does not exist; or, at least, it is unattainable at the present moment. This is why the so-called 'world ethos' remains an abstraction", which has led to "... a necessary relatedness between reason and faith and between reason and religion", where "... in the intercultural context the two main partners in this mutual relatedness are the Christian faith and Western secular rationality".

And in relation to the manner in which reason and religion are related, he considers as follows: "If we have noted the urgent question of whether religion is truly a positive force, so we must now *doubt the reliability of reason*. For in the last analysis, even the atomic bomb is a product of reason; in the last analysis, the breeding and selection of human beings is something thought up by reason. Does this then mean that it is reason that ought to be placed under guardianship? But by whom or by what? Or should perhaps religion and reason restrict each other and remind each other where their limits are, thereby encouraging a positive path? Once again, we are confronted with the question how - in a global society with its mechanisms of power and its uncontrolled forces and its varying views of what constitutes law and morality - an effective ethical conviction can be found with sufficient motivation and vigour to answer the challenges I have outlined here and to help us meet these tests."

Naturally, the probing question Dr. Ratzinger had posed had its basis in philosophical anthropology (33)(38). He had started from "... what man is, whence he comes, and what the goal of his existence is ..." and as a corollary to this, whether it was possible to discover a "formula ... that would embrace the whole world and unite all persons" (cf. Chapter XIII: Core Concepts; (38)). He did not find a contemporary answer to this and fell back on the traditional solution long known in our Western history: reason and religion as a shared and common cross-fertilising basis, not only for our human existence, but equally so for the democratic constitutional state, which he calls the "only pre-political contents of democracy". His discussion is linked to concepts such as "power and law (i.e. positive law), natural law and human rights, reason and religion", but remarkably, all these concepts, with the exception of religion, are explicitly explored in depth, whereas no explanation is given with regard to religion; it is assumed to be sufficiently well-known.

To start with, we may justifiably wonder about the nature and meaning of the terms reason and religion and how they are related. It is all the more important to have an answer to this question because, as stated by Dr. Ratzinger, the role of reason is not without objections: "For ... even the atomic bomb is a product of reason ... the breeding and selection of human beings is something thought up by reason".

But why would religions not have been thought up by reason as well? This would also explain the fact that there are so many different religions in the world (34), which would lead to the conclusion that all religions are of equal standing. Reason, after all, refers to the process of experience by which people lead their lives; it is this process that engenders their religiosity (in a broad sense: spirituality, mysticism, and so on) and their faiths. And then human beings can only stay in equilibrium by using their intellect and taking their responsibility (33).

What are the foundations of a democratic constitutional state?

To my mind, this question revolves around the concept of power, the essence of which term Dr. Ratzinger refrained from formulating. The way I see it, power must be viewed in the light of the question what essential characteristics we ascribe to human beings as absolute entities, which is decisive for the way in which people get along with one another. If we bear these essential characteristics (survival, communication, identity, self-fulfilment and autonomy) in mind, we see that, basically, power and its exercise can only be viewed as a caricature; in other words: any way in which power is exercised that is in conflict with the interests, or against the will, of other people makes the power from which it derives or the person who exercises it a caricature. Such exercise of power must be deemed contrary to the nature of human beings as absolute entities and therefore contrary to their very being and their essential characteristics.

In broader terms, the use of power can be regarded as a form of promotion of interests, and in principle, there can be no objection to this. If people undertake economically motivated activities (for survival purposes), then the power exercised in that context is generally permissible. This changes when we enter the field of communication (the playing field of illusion) and the economic motive does not play a role. This is primarily the case in permanent forms of communication (religion and philosophy, art and culture, science and politics), all of which take place on the playing field of illusion, where no one can claim that their truth is absolute nor can they expect another person to acknowledge it as such.

Specifically, being in a position of power and wielding power have an effect on our relationships with other people, in which there is a role for morals and ethics. It is always a matter between individuals, and all of them work in their own way to promote their own interests. But when they are unable to promote certain of their interests on their own, they will band together, something that takes place in all fields imaginable. When they take this step, human beings as absolute entities step outside of themselves, thus shaping a form of co-existence the nature of which can be both material and immaterial: immaterial because they are driven together by a shared motive, and material when, as a group, they give shape to their collaboration by setting up a range of social institutions. This manner of promoting individual and collective interests knows no bounds, and will always result in the unlimited pursuit of their own interests and the related unbridled exercise of power, which inevitably leads to all manner of social problems. Moreover, it implies an incessant struggle (between individuals) and war (between groups), things people commonly engage in yet today.

People only recently came to understand this, and they developed the concept of a democratic constitutional state, which created a basis for them to live together peacefully. The chief characteristic of a constitutional democracy is that people subject themselves to its regime voluntarily, thus legitimating the power accruing to it as well as the exercise of this power. But there are limits to anything to which people voluntarily subject themselves, and the objectives of a constitutional democracy must largely be in line with promotion of the individual and collective interests of its subjects, on whose support the constitutional democracy must be able to rely. The focus of their interests will primarily be economic (i.e. survival).

Democracy can thus exert its influence on society as a whole as well as on the individual citizens, and the longer it has developed (thus having attained a higher degree of organisation), the more will its influence be felt. The immaterial concept of the constitutional democracy has taken shape in the form of material democratic institutions that are anchored in society. Thanks to the present high organisational level of most Western democracies, nearly all social institutions are amply legitimated and derive their identity from this, allowing them to share some of the state's power and endowing them with certain competencies or powers to act to the exclusion of others (they enjoy exclusivity). Despite the fact that citizens and societal institutions enjoy a large degree of freedom to act as they see fit, government has gained a considerable grip on society as a whole. As a result, it has been able to set limits to competition and rivalry and to power and its exercise (cartels, monopolies, etc.) by means of legislation, and to enforce compliance, if necessary with the use of violence.

Beyond the scope of economic life, and especially on the playing field of illusion (permanent forms of communication), government influence should be kept to a minimum because this is the exclusive domain of individual citizens. It should be reserved to them because it is where they can bring to expression their essential characteristics as absolute entities (communication, identity, self-fulfilment and autonomy), areas in which they ought to be entirely free. Their essential characteristics have therefore acquired an important place within a constitutional democracy in the form of basic rights and freedoms that protect citizens against the power of the state (such as freedom of opinion, of association and meeting, mental and physical integrity and religion). In fact the role of the government can largely be defined as creating the frameworks in which individual citizens can move freely (or as freely as possible).

In a constitutional democracy, for the first time in history people have taken their fate in their own hands. One of their first acts was to create a division between church and state, in which churches are subordinate to the state, so that the power of the state prevails.

The above definition of human beings as absolute entities makes it clear that the way in which they get along with each other is primarily determined by the free interplay of forces. In this respect they can impose limitations on themselves (exercise voluntary self-restraint) in order to keep the peace (obey their conscience) and can avail themselves of norms (rules of morality, ethics and decency) as guidelines for their actions. This concerns the relationship between individuals in contrast to individuals as members of a group (family and friends, clubs, companies, churches, government) where the group imposes standards (rules of morality, ethics and decency, mores, custom and practice, laws) on its participants, who must adhere to them.

From this it can be concluded that the free interplay of forces (absolute freedom) is inherent in human nature, that any limitation is alien to it and that the use of norms is only prompted by a certain need for ordering, depending on the circumstances (i.e. to ensure that norms are effective), when they have conflicting interests. We must distinguish the freedom to realise the totality of all essential characteristics of human beings as absolute entities in relation to others from the relative freedom people have to achieve their autonomy through self-determination, which is limited in this sense.

In this context we might define the term 'world ethos' as total love of yourself and others because we have come to realise that it is the only route to the essential characteristic of self-fulfilment (self-development and the search for meaning) as the ultimate goal of human beings as absolute entities. When we reach that point, we have developed in the sense that we are able to give ourselves and others the scope we need as absolute entities (compassion, solidarity).

2 *Herman Philipse's philosophy and the sciences (2)*

"Philosophers had good reason to reject the presumption that the branches of science are founded on philosophy ..... If we summarise the differences between the old and the new conception of philosophy, we can say that according to the notion of philosophy as a rational world view, the philosopher often takes the sciences as his foundation rather than the other way round, and that he must be modest in his own scientific pretensions", according to Dr. Herman Philipse, Professor of Philosophy at Utrecht University in his *Atheistisch Manifest* in 1995 (to which *De onredelijkheid van religie* and a foreword by Ayaan Hirsi Ali were added in 2004).

In his view, "... the discussion of philosophical problems often requires a considerable degree of scientific knowledge. If one is not familiar with the overall structure of classical mechanics and quantum theory, and perhaps also genetics, chemistry, certain branches of mathematics and the physiology of the brain, one will not be able to put forward anything of significance in relation to the problem of freedom and determinism ..... The scientific attitude requires a number of virtues, such as curiosity, creativity in devising alternative views, recalcitrance, intellectual autonomy, honesty, respect for different opinions, and a willingness to learn from criticism, virtues that, according to the principles of collective hardheadedness, must be regarded as sins ..... children must be taught with great care to adopt a scientific attitude from an early age. This does not mean that a large portion of the population should choose a career in science – only those who excel at the aforementioned virtues. But it does mean that a democratic state must esteem scientific research in a narrow sense, because it leads to the development of a cognitive attitude that can serve as an example to every member of society [but] ... it is also a question of the heart and the imagination, of empathy and of love for others".

He considers "religious beliefs, faith and religion [to be] incompatible with science or reason"; he defines religion scientifically and specifically rejects religious doctrine. He describes reason "... as the whole of methods of empirical scientific research and critical discursive thinking as they have evolved in the scientific tradition and will continue to develop in the future" and he defines "... the phenomenon of conscience as a mental organ that can be scientifically explained and that makes the religious explanation superfluous ...". In his opinion, we "... often must act in accordance with our conscience because otherwise we [would] lose our self-respect ...".

The first thing that can be concluded from the foregoing is that Herman Philipse imposes a hierarchy on a number of things that are equal by nature: he classifies science as the highest in rank, discards religion and sees philosophy, a rational view of the world, as based solely on the sciences. However, what he fails to appreciate is the significance of communication for religion and philosophy, art and culture, science and politics, all of which reveal information about the innermost essence of human beings. His rejection of religious doctrine means that he fails to recognise the role played in this respect by power and the exercise of power. The biggest drawback to religious systems, after all, is not the doctrines themselves, but the hierarchical power structures and rules of life derived from the doctrine, and the accompanying sanctions if they are not adhered to.

When a person exercises power in a way that is contrary to the interests or against the will of others, it makes a caricature of that person's power or the person exercising it. Such exercise of power is contrary to the nature of human beings as absolute entities and therefore contrary to their being and their essential characteristics. Generally speaking, the use of power can be regarded as a form of promotion of interests, and not much objection can be made to this. If people's activities are economically motivated (survival), then the power exercised in that context is generally permissible. This changes when we enter the field of communication (the playing field of illusion) and the economic motive does not play a role. This is primarily the case in permanent forms of communication (religion and philosophy, art and culture, science and politics), all of which take place on the playing field of illusion, where no-one can claim that their truth is absolute nor can they expect another person to recognise it as such.

What is communication and when does it take on a permanent form?

In simple terms, communication is an attempt to connect with another human being. However, a great deal can go wrong, resulting in miscommunication or misunderstandings. In everyday dealings this takes place (incidentally, fleetingly) in our direct contacts with other persons, against a background of economic or simply social reasons (exchange of information (in a broad sense), networking). In relation to the second essential characteristic of human beings as absolute entities (inward-looking (closed); an end in themselves (autonomy, being yourself); isolation and communication (in a broad and immaterial sense)), people communicate for other reasons and this can therefore take place in all other fields in which people are active. Typical of this type of communication is that the content of the message is considerably more complex; direct contact is inadequate for its transfer, so that some other means (indirect, with a more lasting form) must be sought, thus giving communication a permanence in our lives. Texts, textbooks, image and sound recordings are permanent forms of communication. Religion and philosophy, art and culture, science and politics are expressions of this and therefore also belong to the world of the imagination (15).

From this it follows that communication does not truly exist; it is illusory. Communication cannot alter our isolation. The means of communication are expressions of what people experience, of the process of experience that they perceive and of which they are part, that they are themselves (5) (38). They manifest themselves outside the detachment of people in a sort of space that we could term the playing field of illusion, where the exchange takes place, by which the link is made.

We must also make a distinction between forms of communication (the means) and the content of the message they put across. As we have seen, communication entails a fair chance of misunderstanding or miscommunication. This means that, to actually put a message across, the sender must have a clear idea of its contents. The sender must correctly translate the contents of the message into the means of communication of choice, so that the recipient of the message can reasonably be expected to understand it (in an objective sense). The recipient will receive the message via his or her own process of experience, thus colouring the translation, which is now different from the original intention of the sender. The original intention of the sender can be approached more closely by conducting further or more intensive communication until both sender and recipient have the impression that the communication properly reflects the intention.

Communication takes place in phases: it starts in the first phase, the process of experience in the sender, taking place via the playing field of illusion, and ending in the final phase of the process of experience in the recipient. This information flow comprises no end of opportunities that could lead to misunderstanding or miscommunication.

The social skills and intelligence of those who take part play a big role in this respect. So we can ascertain that we are dealing with a complicated process in which there is but a slight chance that the contents of the message will be identical for both sender and recipient.

A clear picture of man does not emerge from Philipse's philosophy (the process of experience, origin and evolution, essential characteristics), nor how people get along with one another (absolute freedom, possessing and exercising power, communication, conscience, morals and ethics) and how they deal with nature, things every philosophy ought to be based on. The starting point is always the process of experience in which human beings are entangled in everyday life. However you look at it, this always remains the basis. It is where everything converges: origin and evolution and essential characteristics that do not really exist, but that can be seen as motives for action that are anchored in an absolute sense in a person's being. A person's objectives are a logical corollary and can then be formulated. They therefore arise directly from man's origin and evolution and are related to his essential characteristics. But this also means that no philosophy can escape answering the most elementary questions of philosophical anthropology because:

"...philosophical anthropology is a domain all its own, and cannot be replaced by any other anthropology. The ultimate explanation of man lies **outside** all possible scientific views that have been formulated, because they lie within the origins of every branch of science, including the science of philosophy. It is the final ground on which the philosophies, of any nature whatsoever, can be pursued implicitly or explicitly", according to the philosopher, theologian and classical scholar Dr. Reinout Bakker, former professor of philosophy, who also "... advocate[s] the necessary collaboration between philosophy and science ... [because] philosophy without contact with the empirical sciences is empty, but also: the empirical sciences are blind without the contribution of philosophy. If one of these two poles is made absolute, there is an imminent danger of gross onesidedness, or even distortion. The fact that the ultimate questions about man are so rarely asked stems from giving the scientific pillar of philosophy an absolute status. Many phenomenologists and existentialists have warned against this scientism ..." (33) (38).

3 Victor Lamme's consciousness

The concept of experience and human beings as absolute entities
A philosophical anthropological approach

"What is needed for consciousness is recurrent interactions, which is to say: something in the brain changes", says Prof. Victor A.F. Lamme, Professor of Cognitive Neurosciences at the University of Amsterdam, and he adds that "... people don't know what they are conscious of" (30). For the success of his research he thinks it is necessary to move our "notion" of "mind" to the "brain", and in this context he speaks of "visual consciousness" (31).

Victor Lamme is evidently one who assumes that consciousness actually exists, in some way or other (13), and that as a term, the word has a corresponding meaning (8). Although in the above description Lamme does state what is needed for consciousness, he does not give a corresponding definition. Furthermore, it is not clear whether his understanding of consciousness means the same as the term "visual consciousness", which he uses in this context.

It is plausible that in his view, visual consciousness is the same as recurrent interactions, by which something in the brain changes; in other words, the operation of the brain is not only responsible for consciousness, but it is consciousness itself. To put it another way, it is the brain that possesses consciousness, and not we ourselves. Compare this to Dick Swaab: "We are our brain" (5). Lamme therefore apparently uses the word consciousness to indicate that the brain is autonomous, that it is outside of our perception and influence (5).

I consider the word consciousness to be ambiguous and extremely confusing in this context because it has led to many controversies in the literature: its existence is denied (5); there are divergent views as to its meaning (8). Terminologically, with his umpteenth variant on the term, Lamme clearly belongs to the latter group. However, in terms of content the word has a meaning that has nothing to do with consciousness (8), but is solely meant to designate the brain's autonomy. After all, as Lamme says, "people don't know what they are conscious of". Only the brain possesses consciousness.

In my philosophy of man I have described experience (perception, cognisance) as the manner in which human beings operate as absolute entities. Experience as a concept can be described as parts, or phases, of processes in the brain. These processes are autonomous (5). Accordingly, experience can be divided into the following parts or phases:

1 Observation (Input)
2 Storage (Memory)
3 Organising (Combining)
4 Conclusion or Finding (Mood, Intuition, Feelings, Emotions, Thought, Knowledge, Comprehension, Idea, Mental Grasp, Consciousness, Mind, Soul, Psyche, Will, Conscience, etc.)
5 Plan
6 Performance (Output)

The following quotes from Lamme (30) show that he draws on all parts of the process of experience as thus described in his considerations, without placing them in a logical order:

"... there is no good definition of consciousness and the object of my research is to give one..."

"... my research is a logical extension of my doctoral research of visual observation (phase 1)..."

"... a new, neurobiological definition in the form of a hypothesis...": "What is needed for consciousness is recurrent interactions (phase 3), which is to say: something in the brain changes."

"... people don't know (phase 4) what they are conscious of..."

"... not the knowledge (phase 4), but the interactions preceding it (phase 3), is the essence of consciousness..."

"... as soon as there are recurrent interactions (phase 3), there is consciousness, even if it is not reportable (phase 6). As soon as a tiny speck of consciousness comes about in the brain, all kinds of things become a part of it: memory (phase 2), emotions (phase 4), form (phase 1, phases 5 + 6), colour (phase 1, phases 5 + 6), movement (phase 1, phases 5 + 6). And at a certain point there is a link to the reporting module (phase 6). This makes it easier to communicate about something (phase 6), but it is not the essence. The essence is the recurrent interactions (phase 3). Then you also understand that consciousness has nothing to do with attention (phase 1), language (phase 6) or button-pushing (phase 6), but that it is all about the creation (phase 3) of memory traces (phase 2)."

(phases added by author)

In the quotations I have inserted the phases of the process of experience to which the words relate, from which it can be deduced that the term recurrent interactions refers to organising (combining) (phase 3), or the exchange of information between the brain cells, which Lamme calls "conscious discussion" (2).

From the meaning of the terms consciousness and recurrent interactions as seen above, it can be deduced that the two are of a completely different order and thus are not the same.

Whatever meaning the terms consciousness and recurrent interactions may have, the foregoing makes it clear that they only take on real significance when they are embedded in the whole of their everyday order of being. This is not Lamme's point of view: he regards his hypothesis solely from his own perspective of cognitive neuroscience, without looking at the broader philosophical anthropological implications. And then it is not surprising that he evidently cannot put his finger on the distinction between human consciousness and a camera. Lamme: "We process visual information, but so does a camera that automatically detects people entering a lift. Surely no one assumes that somewhere something like consciousness is part of such a system. So why do we have it? If we receive a visual stimulus, why do we see it? Why do we have an image before our eyes? No one knows the answer to this question and that is what makes it interesting." (30). The irrefutable answer to this question is that man, the absolute entity, is involved in an empirical experiment but a camera is not.

In this sense, human beings as absolute entities have undergone certain developments over millions of years (they have evolved) so that today we can cite a number of features (essential characteristics) in relation to their nature and origin. In this process our empirical involvement can be regarded as the motor that has made us (caused us to develop) into what we are today. This is our everyday reality. We have deduced our essential characteristics (an urge for survival, communication, identity, self-fulfilment, self-determination) from them alone and they can be seen as the motives - which have proved in the course of history to be enduring - for our actions. They therefore do not truly exist, but they apparently typify our most original state of being, set down in billions of cells (matter) that make us who we are.

The conclusion is therefore that Victor Lamme's hypothesis cannot hold up because, as we have seen, the word consciousness means something different to him than his term recurrent interactions. By pulling the word consciousness into his hypothesis, Lamme is no longer working solely in his own field of cognitive neuroscience; he has also stepped onto the terrain of philosophical anthropology without expressing himself in greater detail on this (45). He merely limits himself to the observation that there "is no good definition of consciousness" and then the term is claimed in the meaning he has given it (from the perspective of cognitive neuroscience). It is all the more confusing when he refers not only to "visual consciousness", but also to "visual observation/information/stimulus" and "seeing" or "having an image before our eyes" as synonyms of "visual consciousness", the accuracy of which must be seriously doubted at the very least.

Lamme knows this too, but is not sufficiently conscious of it: "The more we understand about this subject, the more abstruse becomes the problem of mind-body separation" (2). Quite aside from the philosophical anthropological implications, it is likely that he and his cognitive neurosciences have a long way to go because after all, brain activity "is such a huge network that we will need several generations of information technology to gain even the slightest grasp of it." (Quoted from Prof. Jan van Gijn, note (5), on the relationship of body to mind (8, concluding sentence)).

4 Hans Achterhuis's violence and philosophical anthropology (2)

In his book published in 2008 [*Met alle geweld*], philosopher and emeritus professor Dr. Hans Achterhuis, lacking a "universal definition", defined the word violence as "... more or less intentionally causing or threatening to cause damage to people or objects", which was borrowed from an anthology [*Filosoferen over geweld*] by D. Boeykens. He calls this a descriptive definition that has "normative overtones". It is in any case "not meant in an essentialist sense" because in that case he "... would be trying to indicate the universal essence of violence", which would "require an anthropology and an ontology, a theory on how human beings work in their deepest innermost beings". By contrast, he would "... prefer not to diverge from the fact that violence is definitely a historic concept and that in the course of history, its definition and the value judgment entailed may have seen marked changes".

His philosophical anthropological considerations would lead one to conclude that he is among the philosophers who question the right to exist of philosophical anthropology (3) and are of the opinion that its task, finding the fundamental human truth, has been taken over by the sciences (2). He specifically cites "... Helmuth Plessner [Germany, 1892-1985; author], who more and more tends to be considered the founder and uncrowned king of philosophical anthropology ... [and] is even often classed as a 'philosophical biologist'". Then, after discussing his philosophy in broad lines, he concludes that "... this biologist, despite his great attention to empiricism, nevertheless ends up a more or less traditional metaphysicist ... if we are to make his work productive for a new understanding of nature, it will have to be thoroughly reviewed and added to".

The final conclusion is therefore that for his subject, Hans Achterhuis "... primarily cites biologists, ethologists and evolutionary psychologists with a philosophical interest" because "they presently have more to offer [him] than do his immediate colleagues". Furthermore, "... it will be clear that ethologists and sociobiologists are of the opinion that the violent behaviour of human beings must be understood in part from the point of view of the evolutionary history of the sort..... most philosophers and philosophical anthropologists are not aware of this. Their considerations suggest that violence only entered our world together with humankind."

I do not concur in Achterhuis's choice of a "historic concept of violence" because, under the circumstances he put forward, he should at least have investigated whether it was reasonably possible to formulate "the universal essence of violence" and "an anthropology and an ontology, a theory on how human beings work in their innermost essence". In the affirmative case the concept of violence could be anchored in the foundations of human existence and thus could have taken on the meaning with the widest scope, whereas his definition lacks any such firm basis and therefore can be called one-sided, arbitrary - a concept the meaning of which depends on time, place and circumstances, or in his own words "… that its definition and the value judgment entailed may have seen marked changes in the course of history".

In my philosophy of man, violence is essentially connected with conscience and the other, in relation to a conflict of interests. It must be stated first and foremost that human beings as absolute entities are completely free (they have absolute freedom) in the manner in which they achieve their objectives. In this context, violence can only be seen as a means by which to allow our own interests to take precedence over the interests of others by forcing others to promote our interests. Violence, whatever its nature and scope and whatever its consequences (28), is in this context no more than a means of power used between two or more parties and is therefore without a relevant substantive meaning.

In this sense violence is not "the more or less intentionally causing or threatening to cause damage to people or objects", but merely one of the means by which we promote our own interests, the use of which we can also choose to refrain from. Conscience (moral and ethical) is at issue here; the question a person asks is: how shall I deal with the interests involved? Achterhuis's definition of violence is simply the greatest common denominator of a summary of the many types of violence that have existed through the ages on the basis of a meaning he has attributed to the word; it does not have its origin in the foundations of human existence because it cannot be traced back to the essential characteristics of human beings as absolute entities (urge for survival, communication, identity, self-fulfilment, autonomy).

At the beginning of his monumental work, Achterhuis asks himself "What is the counterpart of violence?" To him, "'non-violence' is not an adequate answer", but he does not discuss this explicitly in the rest of his work. To my mind, the use of violence should be treated simply as the violent method of promotion of interests, in contrast to the non-violent method which might also be termed the peaceable method, based on a presumed equality of the parties and where their mutual interests are promoted through consultation and negotiation, i.e. by means of communication without the use of power. The counterpart to violence sought by Achterhuis can then be found in the words 'without violence' or 'non-violent action'. From this point of view, the word non-violence means systematically refraining from the use of violence in promoting one's interests. The use of force can be said to produce forceful behaviour, in contrast to non-forceful.

One of the chief ways in which violence occurs in everyday life is hidden or veiled in our communications without us being aware of it. Communication uses language (verbal), images (non-verbal) and sound (voice) or a combination of these, or certain forms of conduct. To communicate without violence (29), it is important to focus your consciousness on this by observing accurately (what do you see?) and not judging (what do you feel or think?), but only putting forward hard facts. Violence as referred to here is ubiquitous and forms an obstacle to an efficient promotion of interests; it is one of the most significant manifestations of violence. By focusing more consciously on this, we make ourselves morally accountable and allow our conscience to speak, on the basis of respect for and compassion with another person and their interests. What it turns on here is speaking 'with your heart' and not 'with your head', by which you show that you are connected with yourself; then the other person will feel approached on an equal footing.

Rather more alarming is the fact that in Achterhuis's view, violence is inherent in human nature. Where Achterhuis rejects a universal definition on the one hand, through the backdoor he nevertheless advances an important essentialist characteristic, in his view perhaps the most important characteristic of human beings. To my mind, human beings are certainly not violent by nature; quite the contrary. In principle they are free to make moral choices and to take responsibility. A corollary to Achterhuis's view is that aggression and violence cannot be unlearned, not even by focusing on it consciously. Being a great deal more optimistic, I am of the opinion that a lot can be achieved in this sense. In my opinion, this is only not the case when we are dealing with people with a personality problem or problems of a psychopathological nature. Living our lives deliberately and consciously, being disciplined, educating ourselves and our children is therefore very much worthwhile; it will enable us to resolve the problems that occur in life in a peaceable (non-violent) manner, and if each of us does so consistently, it ought to be possible to achieve permanent peace (non-violence) in the world.

Finally, the quotations from Professor Bakker (3) below show that Achterhuis is correct as to the impasse in which philosophical anthropology finds itself at present, but as to the alternative he chooses (the sciences, more specifically sociobiology and ethology) the two men are miles apart, which he follows with an urgent appeal for philosophical reflection:

"Reviewing the anthropologists discussed [Scheler, Gehlen and Plessner; author], then we see that biology as an empirical science is an inadequate way of interpreting human beings. The three thinkers leave behind remnants that cannot be divvied up over purely scientific categories". "... Plessner centres his anthropology around the eccentricity of human beings, a category that ... defies empirical investigation ..... A comparison of humans to animals is not very productive because human beings are always the subject of the comparison".

"The paralysing uncertainty of the future, not knowing where we are going and where we will be when we get there, the loss of the authority of values and norms and scepticism of the teleology of history leave no doubt that it makes sense to reactualise philosophical anthropology in a joint philosophical reflection".

"Just as human beings are more than the sum of their parts, so is philosophical anthropology more than the sum of everything the sciences have thought or said about human beings. And philosophical anthropology is also about this 'more'!" (33).

5 East and West are one world (11)

Or: How T'ai Chi Ch'uan and Voice Dialogue International form an energetic connection between East and West (25)

For years, people have been looking for a "theory of everything", one with which the assumed or hoped-for fundamental unity can be explained (10), but so far without success. The question remains whether one will ever be found, and in the negative case we will have to be satisfied with what there is, no more and no less; surely it is unproductive to speculate about our existence without any basis.

In our evolution (our common origin) I named the cosmos as the first known and irrefutable part. Although I did not define it in further detail, its characteristics are: intelligence (plan, order, structure), energy, form and matter. The concept of energy was briefly discussed in the consideration of the first characteristic of human beings as absolute entities, namely our dependence and urge for survival, which is of a material nature. How this energy occurs is briefly explained, but nowhere is the question addressed of what constitutes energy. Our discussion of the way in which energy manifests itself warrants the conclusion that energy is omnipresent. Energy is everywhere, but what it is remains shrouded in mystery. I will come back to this.

T'ai Chi is one of the many Eastern introspective arts that have existed for centuries; it is a complete route to self-development, in which lifeforce is stimulated and nourished. It comprises both gentleness and strength (25). In the 1970s, an American psychologist couple, Dr. Hal Stone and Dr. Sidra Stone, developed the Voice Dialogue method (26). It is a technique which allows you to enter into a dialogue with your inner voices, also termed sub-personalities or energy systems. The basic principle of both T'ai Chi and Voice Dialogue is therefore life energy.

One of the most important disciples of the Stones is Robert Stamboliev (27). He studied at Utrecht University and William Lyon University in San Diego, California under Dr. Hal Stone and was involved in Voice Dialogue at a very early stage. He gained his MA in Transformational Psychology in 1988 with a paper published in revised form under the title of *The Energetics of Voice Dialogue* (25) under the auspices of the Institute for

Transformational Psychology (ITP) in Bergen, the Netherlands (26). In this book "... the energetic aspects of the Voice Dialogue method are explored and explained in further detail ...", leading to "greater insight into the energetic principles".

In their foreword to this edition, Hal and Sidra Stone praise his "... exceptional skills as a teacher and trainer ..." and observe that "... by building further on his broad background in Tai Chi ... [he] succeeded in making the link between his knowledge of Energetics and his own insight into and experience with Voice Dialogue and the theory of the 'selves'".

Voice Dialogue, they say, "... is not a system in itself and within itself. Because it is both a method and a philosophical approach to consciousness [(5)], Voice Dialogue can be integrated in almost every system, both methodologically and theoretically. And this is exactly what is now happening all over the world. Robert has developed his own unique style for coaching, knowledge transfer and training, and the core of his work lies in his experience with and knowledge of energetic processes."
Robert Stamboliev is portrayed by his teachers as a great bridge builder between the Eastern philosophies and the Western sciences viewed from the shared field of energetics. His Institute of Transformational Psychology has made a significant contribution to the propagation and application of Voice Dialogue in the world (26).

What is so special about Voice Dialogue?

What is so special about Voice Dialogue? It helps an ego to become aware of energy patterns (sub-personalities) by conducting a dialogue with each of them individually, thus allowing all of them to move into harmony with one another so that people can make conscious choices.

The subject and the coach are on an equal footing; the coach even plays the role of the subject and therefore undergoes the same consciousness process as he or she does. Conversely, the subject can also be asked to play the role of coach. Consciousness explicitly does not refer to "the essential Self", but to the Aware Ego process, which is independent, neutral and reflective (5).

The ego, the sub-personalities and the aware ego process are viewed as each residing in separate physical spaces. The sub-personalities are divided into primary selves with which we are identified (protector/controller (= basic energy), pleaser, pusher, inner critic and perfectionist) and disowned selves, our buried instinctive energies that continually come at us in our dreams as disowned energy patterns (the vulnerable child). The idea is that the investigation (the dialogue) exposes the primary selves, after which the person can dis-identify himself (move away) and the disowned selves can then manifest themselves.

As a process, my philosophical anthropological approach to the process of experience can be likened to the aforementioned process of awareness and consciousness; it too is not a single process, but many of them. Like family constellations, Voice Dialogue is about observation and communication (26). The processes described by Robert Stamboliev are certainly comparable to the paranormal events that we see in Bert Hellinger's therapy. The shared field and the collective soul of the latter can surely be likened to the vibrating energies or energy fields (electromagnetic fields) in which Stamboliev immerses himself or to which he yields, or for which the right place must be occupied, and the auras (energy fields of the body) and chakras (energy centres) that he evidently is able to see.

In this context I would like to advocate broadening the concept of experience (observation) and carrying out further research. The concepts I use in this context, goal and interest, and in connection with them, motivation, play an important role. Sub-personalities can be regarded as interest promoters for the achievement of the objectives in accordance with our essential characteristics as absolute entities. In this context, promoter of interests is not meant in a material (substantive) sense (the interest itself and its promotion); what is important is the form it takes (the manner in which this is done, or by whom).

The axioms named by Stamboliev in connection with the concept of energy are interesting: energy can be guided and directed (it follows thoughts), it is inductive (it can be transferred without words or touch; there is a relationship with resonance) and neutral.

To me, it is simply spectacular that Voice Dialogue can be applied locally, regionally and culturally. Hal Stone gives a fascinating example of disowning energy patterns at a cultural level: "Western civilization, for example, has created the seven deadly sins.

Who among us has not been encouraged at one time or another to do away with pride, covetousness, lust, anger, gluttony, envy and sloth? Since the Age of Enlightenment humanity has disowned all the “darker” energies - the passionate, the irrational, the mystical, the unclear and the paradoxical - and admired, almost worshipped, rationality, detachment, scientific objectivity, and clarity. In this way, we have negated much of the information available to us as human beings. We have also negated our anger, irritability, insecurities and confusions in favor of balance, good humor, certainty, and self-confidence. The disowning of “the seven deadly sins” results in a particular build-up of instinctual energies in the unconscious that we call demonic energies. They are among the major disowned energy patterns, and as a society we pay a particularly heavy price for their negation.” (26)(28).

6 Bert Hellinger's family constellations (23)

The concept of experience and human beings as absolute entities
With reference to an article by G.A. Terpstra in Wijsgerig Perspectief (24)

In his article in *Wijsgerig Perspectief* Terpstra attempted to give Hellinger's family constellation a broader philosophical basis. Hellinger's writings and the literature about his work paint a solid picture of the family constellation and the role of those involved in it: the client's representative, representatives of family members and last but not least, the therapist. The subtitle of one of his books states the purpose of the family constellation in a nutshell: "Instrument for Conflict Management". This route ultimately brings us to psychoanalysis.

As I read his books, I observed that Hellinger is reputed to be an empiricist and existentialist. His "philosophical companion" is Martin Heidegger (Germany 1889-1976), one of the founders of existentialism, which focuses on 'concrete being'. This is precisely what I have attempted to describe in my philosophy of man, without pretending or even wanting to be an existentialist. And so I was very surprised to discover that Bert Terpstra approaches the family constellation from a totally different angle: based on the philosophy of Paul Feyerabend (Austria/USA 1924-1994), which is the philosophy of science. To my mind, a theory or a philosophy quickly becomes incomprehensible if the simple everydayness of concrete human existence is not part of its considerations; this is an aspect I miss in many philosophers and to be honest, in Terpstra and Feyerabend as well.

Some of the terms they use - "being" that is "not known immediately" and "reality" as "phenomena" of "being" - are far removed from everyday reality. And how to construe this: "interaction between people (for example, the family constellation) with being which may, although does not necessarily, lead to a response of being". Terpstra bases his ideas on two pillars, science and art. In relation to art, I am unable to form a meaningful conception of the terms he uses ("reality and illusions in gradations") in which illusions are not true illusions, but in fact more like reality. To him, the Greek gods really existed in the life of the Greeks and "cannot be put aside as illusions". I find his scientific arguments debatable. It is my understanding that the string theory has long since supplanted the quantum theory as a candidate for a "theory of everything" (10), but has itself become an object of criticism. Terpstra, however, seems to assume that the quantum theory is widely accepted. I expect it will take some time before our grasp of this subject becomes clear, if indeed it ever is to be.

To my mind family constellations have much more to do with observation and communication, and revolve around the concept of experience and the way in which we exchange information with each other. In this context, the meaning of words becomes very important. For example, ninety percent of neuroscientists equate experience with sensory perception; they think it does not include thought (or consciousness), and that thought and consciousness represent a separate category located in several places in the brain (13). In my opinion, both are part of the same process (i.e. experience in a broad sense).

I am more inclined to qualify what Hellinger does as paranormal phenomena (8) (cf. clairvoyance, clairsentience and clairaudience), as forms of observation. We might liken it to dreams, visions and apparitions. To my mind, it has its basis in our brain and our five senses (or is it six?!). Here too, the best approach seems to me to seek and widen the boundaries of the concept of experience; from this perspective, the therapist's observations of the family constellation become normal (as opposed to paranormal). But this will require investigating just how this observation takes place, which will be no easy matter. Furthermore, it will meet with resistance from the 'sciences'.

In a family constellation, it is extremely difficult to monitor the role of the representatives and other family members, meaning it cannot be determined objectively. In all constellations described, Hellinger is clearly the pivotal organiser; he is in complete charge of the situation, he runs the game and although I always get the feeling that he is right, I am also inclined to see him as the facilitator, the monopoly holder of the system. Not many will match him!

In his explanations in retrospect and his answers to questions, what he says is very understandable. It offers a glimpse into that so interesting world referred to by him as the shared field and the collective soul, where the order of love prevails. The peace and calm he has given to large groups of people all over the world by helping them share their sorrow with one another I find particularly heart-warming. It is what I wish for every one of us!

7 Experience creates desire and makes us happy

Letter to Arnon Grunberg

Dear Arnon Grunberg

Your philosophical considerations "on the writer George Steiner" entitled *Thinking Leads to Sadness; Ten Reasons Why our Consciousness Generates Sorrow* (35) give me reason to make a few comments.

2500 years of philosophy have not brought us any closer to the truth and we can go on in the same way for many years to come; we are not really getting anywhere. What George Steiner did is essentially the same as what all the great thinkers did: they sought the truth outside of themselves instead of drawing themselves into it. And it is logical that this makes him sad. Isn't it about time to focus our eyes on ourselves and see the world from there? George Steiner would have discovered that he had arrived in the world of the imagination, where there are no boundaries, and he would surely have felt more comfortable.

Steiner focuses completely on what he calls thinking, consciousness (which is in itself limited), and this, he says, makes people sad. This focus makes him the prisoner of his own thoughts, which I find rather short-sighted! After all, instead of starting from thinking and consciousness, you could also start from the much broader area of experience. Experience is much broader because it refers to a multitude of processes, of which Steiner's thought is but a small part. Experience can be regarded as the way in which all people in this world are equipped, the compass that shows them the way in the here and now.

From our history of experience we can conclude that people are isolated because they are closed, but also that they would do almost anything to break out of it, and this is only possible by means of communication, with which we enter the world of the imagination. Or in other words, the experience of isolation leads to an irrepressible tendency to break out of it, which automatically brings us to the world of our dreams and fantasies, the world in which everything is possible and permissible, the world where there are no boundaries. In my opinion, this can make us very happy, but in order to get there you must have the right perspective on yourself and that world, which is precisely what is absent in Steiner. Poor man!

What bothers me most about this is that I cannot avoid the impression that you follow Steiner in this respect, apparently without something inside you that rebels against it - which I surely would not have expected of a literary prize winner. At the end of your article the truth comes out: according to Steiner, the sorrow generated by our consciousness brings us to adopt a melancholy attitude to life as a condition for a tolerant agnosticism, which you translate as ironic maturity. From this not only can we deduce that you agree with the ten reasons named (and it is a fact that they all have to do with our isolation and the ensuing limitations: communication), but that you also share the conclusion he links to this: thinking (i.e. its limitations) not only makes us sad, but indeed, ought to lead to self-derision and tongue-in-cheek self-deprecation.

As you will have gathered by now, in my view, the experience of our isolation leads to an irrepressible tendency to break out of this, which automatically brings us into the world of the imagination. We do not need to make any efforts for this. I cannot imagine a more beautiful world and am convinced that our opinions in this respect do not differ. But I am also of the opinion that cause (the limitations of thinking make us sad) and effect (self-derision and self-deprecation) as concluded by Steiner, with which you seem to agree, are not related. After all, our self-derision or self-deprecation is not due to the fact that the nature of thought is too limited and thus makes us sad, but it is exclusively related to the fact that in the world of the imagination no-one owns the truth, which means that all ideas matter, at least in the eyes of their creator - that is all - so that all ideas deserve respect. As do the ideas of Steiner. Self-derision or self-deprecation is completely uncalled for because it is the stopper for the bottle of arrogance.

In fact the only conclusion I see is that we must praise to the skies the creator of our isolation. Because where would we be without our dreams and fantasies? Imagine such a world, one in which there was no such thing as isolation. The only way I can possibly imagine this is after our passing, when we have returned to dust and become part of that great universe that we cannot imagine and that nevertheless strikes fear and terror into our hearts. Might this not be related to the saying: ‘money can’t buy happiness’? We don’t know, but what we do know for certain is that there is nothing more painful for us than to have to say farewell to this world on our way to that unknown state in which we will surely no longer able to experience, let alone think and harass each other with all those lovely ideas.

The other wild ideas of Steiner that you discuss I will not touch on here, but I cannot escape the conclusion that they too - after my foregoing explanation, how could it be otherwise - at the very least, come across as rather contrived. In my opinion he hopelessly intermingles history with his own fantasies into an inextricable tangle that leads nowhere, but which could put the guileless on the wrong track - always a very risky business.

Yet honesty compels me to admit that my own account contributes just as much to the discussion as does Steiner's, as does your own involvement (or at least admiration). We can say for certain that we have allowed ourselves to be touched by it and to take from it what suited us, thus enriching ourselves, which is something that we cannot cherish intensely enough and long enough because it can make us happy!

From the Sublime
Your obedient servant

II Foreword

Philosophical anthropology is the basis of philosophy and thus the foundation of our human lives (33) (Dialogues 1) (38) (47). Throughout the centuries philosophers have attempted to devise a consistent system that would bring the truth to light. The object of study was always the world around us, and in their endless search for the absolute truth, many people invented a divine dimension on the basis of which all of life was explained. Numerous philosophies and religions were invented in this way, beliefs on which people could base their lives. For centuries people have killed one another because they felt that their truth was the absolute truth.

But they forgot that all these ideas were things they had invented themselves, and that if there are several absolute truths, they are all patently false. And still they continue yet today to maintain that they are right and to wage their battles. The philosophers have since discovered that there is no such thing as truth, absolute or otherwise, and that everyone must seek and find his or her own truth in this world (22). The visual arts have willingly allowed themselves to be annexed and have managed to manoeuvre themselves into the domain of philosophy (1). A similar fate will befall philosophica anthropology. Contemporary philosophers make it no secret that philosophical anthropology is up a blind alley and that the sciences have taken over its task, which is finding the fundamental human truth (2). They no longer have any illusions as to the point of having a philosophical anthropology and have resigned themselves to the fact that the vacuum will simply not be filled (3).

One might well say that we have thus arrived at a complete impasse, whereas the need for something to save the situation has become quite urgent at this point in human history. The deep human yearning for an overall vision, one describing a coherent idea about mankind's fundamental state of being that could give life a new basis, makes itself very strongly felt at present. The cause of this crisis is the loss of traditional certainties and the non-emergence of new ones in combination with a total preoccupation with materialistic self-enrichment, thus nipping in the bud the development of new spiritual life. The solution must be found in totally letting go of old prejudices and completely opening our minds to new developments while at the same time practising discipline and soberness, so as to create scope for this (4). In the firm belief that together we can surely arrive at new insights, we must all engage in a dialogue so as to find them.

My philosophy of man is a hypothetical impetus in that direction, and it could well serve as an initiative to achieve this objective. The most important difference in the way the subject is approached is that philosophical anthropology basically looks at human beings themselves (5) and not outside of them, as most thinkers do (6), to explain human life. This makes it possible to better fathom the process of experience as the basis for every human life and to link conclusions to this in relation to the origin and evolution of human beings as well as their essential characteristics; from there we can then reason further towards more mundane topics.

III How it works

Introduction

The entire world population can be regarded as billions of people who went before us in carrying out their assigned task of begetting progeny. The earth is now populated by a great many more people than when we were born. Apparently people are only too happy to do this work. Men and women are indeed so equipped that it is evidently the idea that we make continual attempts. There is always a good chance that one will be successful.

After all, one ejaculation, with a volume of two to five cubic centimetres, contains from 75 to 600 million sperm cells per cubic centimetre. The ovaries, two organs about the size of a walnut and symmetrically situated just below the navel against the side of the pelvis, contain around 50,000 egg cells, which are already present but unripe in the foetus. Until puberty, these egg cells do not develop, but after the onset of menstruation one egg cell ripens every month. This takes place in the Graafian or vesicular follicle, which grows bulges on the surface of the ovary until one ruptures, thus releasing the oocyte. This is called ovulation and generally takes place halfway through the menstrual cycle (7). Just so you know. The general idea is that a single egg cell is penetrated by a single sperm cell, resulting in new life.

A considerable portion of life is focused on the free and unfettered progress towards this development. But is this the only objective of our lives, the most important one? You might almost think so, were it not that newborn life is very vulnerable and dependent, so provisions have to be made for this. Although many children die young, all over the world, billions of people have managed to emerge from the struggle unscathed. Many people concern themselves with the fate of the neonate and organise their lives around this. It is not easy, but by trial and error, people often manage to bring the new life into a state in which it too can take part in this cyclic process.

Semen largely consists of a liquid that nourishes the sperm cells and that is rich in fructose for this purpose. Fructose is a sugar with a simple chemical structure (simple sugar); it is also an ingredient of cane sugar (7). I will not discuss further the physical and chemical composition of the sperm cells and egg cells. But it has been established that they are composed of basic elements found in all human beings. They can be regarded as the germ of all life. Although life appears to us in a physical form, these elements potentially make us who we are; they are the germinal beginnings of our external and internal manifestation. So it is life itself that we have been carrying with us for millions of years. And if Darwin was right, then billions of years ago it was just a tiny fish. If we go on reasoning consistently, that fish might simply have come from the earth itself, which in its turn might have arisen from the Milky Way galaxy, the universe, the cosmos. But then what? In my view, it stops there. These are questions that cannot be answered, and there is no point in speculating about them.

In addition, following this reasoning you saddle yourself with another problem. It arouses the suggestion that time is something with a real existence, while there are a great many reasons to assume that time does not exist, but is merely a human dimension. After all, time implies a beginning and an end, which means it is finite. And finite is the opposite of infinite, of eternity and immortality, which calls up a lot of questions to which there is no answer. From our history we can conclude that this has created a problem for us, one that we do not know how to deal with, but that nevertheless demands a solution to explain the entire phenomenon of life. We are apparently unable to let go of this situation and simply to assume that we are dealing with a state of being, and then to analyse it.

Another insoluble problem created by time is the suggestion that we go through a process of development towards a certain objective, which is something we want, because life without a purpose means life without meaning, without any point. In which case, just what are we doing here! We have been pondering this problem for centuries, and have always had to resort to artifice to find a solution that was somehow satisfactory.

Unfortunately, this same artifice has always caused the way we view our everyday earthly existence to become clouded, distorted, false. If we distance ourselves from time, it does not mean that life has no object and therefore no purpose. It means that we no longer allow time to push us from one thing to the next, that we can lean back into our selves and relax, from this vantage point to see what experiences befall us. Then the sky will clear of its own accord, and what we then see might be very interesting.

One consequence of this theorem is that the Darwinian process of evolution does not necessarily imply that our development is progressive - that we are on our way to improving the species, whatever that may mean. It means that the matter of which we are made can appear in many different manifestations, depending on the circumstances, but it also means that the basis is invariable, that it exhibits characteristics of being that form the actual foundation for our existence. Then it no longer makes any difference who you are or where you are, because time and place are not important. We are all part of one and the same thing (11). Hereditary traits have been passed on unchanged since time immemorial. This applies to all life forms.

So it is not necessarily the case that our development describes a straight line with a beginning and an end, but neither does it mean that our development follows the movement of a circle, an eternally repetitive evolution. Taking our distance from time and place in an absolute sense means that we restrict ourselves merely to our essence, that we can investigate and analyse the characteristics of our essence of which we can be reasonably sure that they exist in some form (44). The most recent developments in the natural sciences, and in quantum theory in particular (10), might well form the basis for this.

Absolute entity

All life forms can be referred to by this concept. To a greater or lesser degree, they all exhibit its characteristics. Its main characteristics are a common origin, a shared evolution and structure. The common origin and the shared evolution mean that all absolute entities are brought in line with their common origin and are also directly connected to it. Absolute entities are structured so as to be ends in themselves, solely focused on self-fulfilment and therefore fully autonomous. Human beings are therefore also absolute entities, and we will limit our discussion to them.

All absolute entities are part of one and the same thing (11). For discussion purposes we divide it into parts, phases, qualities, and so on merely to clarify, but this cannot alter the underlying unity. It therefore follows that all characteristics are interchangeable, that they are all interrelated and that every line of reasoning necessarily leads to the same conclusion.

The words absolute and entity are interrelated, they necessarily complement one another; in this context they cannot be seen as separate from one another, but they also have their own meaning. The word absolute means the absolute, something entirely on its own, without any relationship to anything outside of it. The word entity means essential existence, something that is substantial, a reality or essence. The term absolute entity could therefore be defined as an autonomous unit in itself, but also in relation to its origin, and is therefore the same as the characteristic of being (11).

The origin and evolution of human beings as absolute entities can be divided into five distinctive segments:

1 Cosmos, which cannot be defined, but which has the following characteristics: Intelligence (Plan, Order, Structure), Energy, Form and Matter
2 Planet Earth and Nature (Laws of Nature)
3 Human Beings: Brain, Male and Female, Reproductive Urge
4 Conception (Insemination), Duality, Birth
5 Unity, Absolute Entity

The defining essential characteristics of human beings as absolute entities are:

1 Dependency and Urge for Survival (Material)
2 Inward-looking (Closed), Goal in Itself (Autonomy, Being Yourself), Isolation and Communication (Broad and Immaterial)
3 Identity (Singularity, Character) and Individuality
4 Ultimate Objective: Self-Fulfilment (Development, Search for Meaning)
5 Autonomy (Self-Determination) and Freedom (Relative Freedom)

As absolute entities, human beings operate by means of experience. The concept of experience can be described as parts, or phases, of processes in the brain. These processes are autonomous. Accordingly, experience can be divided into the following parts or phases:

1 Observation (Input)
2 Storage (Memory)
3 Organising (Combining)
4 Conclusion or Finding (Mood, Intuition, Feelings, Emotions, Thought, Knowledge, Reason, Idea, Mental Grasp, Consciousness, Mind, Soul, Psyche, Will, Conscience, etc.)
5 Plan
6 Performance (Output)

If we just let these distinctions sink in, no-one will doubt their existence, at least at first sight. It all sounds perfectly reasonable and we may therefore assume it to be true (33) (44).

But upon closer inspection, you could ask yourself what these words actually mean, and what is behind them, or what terrain the words themselves cover. Although we will always be somewhat in the dark in this respect, it does show us how important it is that we know the correct meaning of words and that we continually ask ourselves if appearances are deceptive. People are always developing and their insights continually changing, so it is of great importance that the meaning of words is continually geared to situations with the most refined precision.

Another aspect that plays a role in this connection is the issue of what people can know: theories of knowledge. But by decoupling the time-space dimension and by focusing on our state of being, this problem can be deemed to have been eliminated. For this discussion, I assume that, now or in the future, we will be able to clarify our deepest essence. I am going to make an attempt at this right now.

And if the distinctions cited above should prove to be based on truth, and therefore can be assumed to be certain, then the conclusion seems justified that they apply to all people all over the world, that is to say to the deepest essence of all people, stripped of their different cultural properties.

The origin and evolution of human beings as absolute entities

The origin and evolution of human beings as absolute entities can be divided into five distinctive segments:

1 Cosmos, which cannot be defined, but has the following characteristics: Intelligence (Plan, Order, Structure), Energy, Form and Matter
2 Planet Earth and Nature (Laws of Nature)
3 Human Beings: Brain, Male and Female, Reproductive Urge
4 Conception (Insemination), Duality, Birth
5 Unity, Absolute Entity

The distinctions made in this context can all be regarded as conditions for the origin, evolution and survival of human beings as absolute entities. The order in which they are named is somewhat hierarchical (from part one to part five), but on the other hand there is also some reciprocity on account of their shared origin. And in this sense, all parts together therefore form a unity (11). They are part of the same tapestry, of one and the same thing. If one of the parts is lost, the unity is broken and this would mean the end of the absolute entity.

The fact that all parts together form a unity does not mean that they cannot each be seen as unities in their own right. This means it is possible to discuss the unity, the absolute entity, with its own essential characteristics. In this discussion, it is of great importance to bear in mind the perspective (they are one and the same), which implies that the essential characteristics of the absolute entity must mesh with the conditions for their origin and evolution, because they are part of it and are aligned with it (11).

Human beings as absolute entities

Here too, the individual essential characteristics can be viewed as independent units, but together they are inextricably bound up and as such they form the unity of absolute entity. They influence one another but are not in a hierarchical relationship; one does not arise from the other. They have independent meaning and operate independently. This is because the factors that determine the essential character of human beings as absolute entities can be regarded as their essentials, i.e. all of them together and each of them separately determine our essence. And their essence is that which makes them what they are, that which distinguishes them one from the other, and therefore touches on their raison d'être.

If the foregoing is correct, then this would mean that the highest priority for every human being is, as early as possible, to focus on the totality of his or her essential characteristics, to reflect on them and more particularly, to align and coordinate all of them with each other - in other words, to achieve equilibrium, and thus to safeguard his or her existence. A pressing question in this context is to what extent people owe something to one another. An argument in favour of this might be found in their common origin and in the consequence of the second essential characteristic: the fundamental need to break out of their isolation.

Apart from this, it can now be postulated that today's human beings are seriously remiss in two respects: in respect of the environment and in respect of the search for meaning or spirituality, both of which are related to the conditions for the survival of planet earth, of nature and its laws, as well as the essential characteristics of selffulfilment as the ultimate goal of development and the search for meaning. You could say that we have lost our way in these respects and that only an in-depth reflection on our innermost essence can point us in the direction of ourselves again. The two are interconnected and are related to the enormous developments of the past centuries, which have resulted in economies of scale, something we now refer to as globalisation, meaning that all developments all over the world influence everything and everyone everywhere. Thanks to recent developments in the field of internet and telephony (communication), we can share our joint concerns with one another and bring them to a solution. For this it is necessary that we reflect on what our essential characteristics entail and bring them into harmony with one another.

The defining essential characteristics of human beings as absolute entities

The defining essential characteristics of human beings as absolute entities are:

1 Dependency and Urge for Survival (Material)
2 Inward-looking (Closed), Goal in Itself (Autonomy, Being Yourself), Isolation and Communication (Broad and Immaterial)
3 Identity (Singularity, Character) and Individuality
4 Ultimate Objective: Self-Fulfilment (Development, Search for Meaning)
5 Autonomy (Self-Determination) and Freedom (Relative Freedom)

1 Dependency and Urge for Survival (Material)

Central to this is our material state of being. On the one hand, material refers to wants, needs, imperfections, death and on the other hand to their obviation by endeavouring to make provisions, to satisfy needs, bring perfection and life. It is from this antithesis that our urge for survival arises. Survival means maintaining living matter on pain of the occurrence of its opposite, dead matter. But this opposition is less absolute than we might think and has only one human dimension. After all, here a link seems to exist to our cosmic condition for existence, of which matter is a characteristic part. And our urge for survival (our will to live) can only be explained by matter that is not merely physical, but also includes, nay bears in itself, our will to live in a form or a manner that we call energy. Matter is therefore not only substance and our visible manifestation, but also embodies energy, which is incorporeal, immaterial, invisible to us. If this energy is the basis of our urge for survival, it is related to what we call intelligence, and then the conclusion would be justified that in an absolute sense matter includes not only energy, but also intelligence. These three quantities bear in them one another's characteristics and in this way they are each other's equals, but viewed from our human dimension it is plausible that they are related hierarchically and that intelligence manifests itself in the form of energy, which appears to us as matter.

However this may be, our first task is to maintain our physical, corporeal essence, but this also leads to the biggest problems. Because we are not self-supporting in this respect, but dependent on the possibilities offered to us by nature, to which all life forms belong, we are obliged to spend a considerable portion of our lives on it. This means using scarce energy to achieve our objectives. To maintain our energy levels, we must spend an average of one-third of our life sleeping. For this, we need a place to live. On average, another one-third of our life is spent acquiring nourishment and a place to live. This leaves one-third for our private life, a considerable portion of which is needed for activities that are directly and indirectly related to our material self-preservation. This means that we are always short of time and always carry on an unrelenting struggle for existence. Not only our own inner struggle, but an external one as well in which we must compete with others, imply that means of existence are scarce. This necessity of the struggle applies not only to individuals, but to the entire world population, which is why nations wage war on one another.

The implication is that our urge for survival is inherent, that everything is permissible, that we are a law unto ourselves; it is a matter of survival of the fittest, and this consequence can manifest itself in all conceivable and inconceivable variants. This situation is recorded in the lower strata of our lives, and it seems very remote in our present day and age because human societies have been created on the basis of rules which can be enforced, if necessary with the use of violence; but the threat will always be there, and even though the rules are enforced, a great many situations are conceivable that can escape the effects of enforcement, and thus the fundamental principle is always applicable.

We might well ask ourselves whether it is a good thing for people as absolute entities to seize every opportunity to raise the level of prosperity all over the world so that a great many people benefit from it. What will be the consequences? We would do well to wonder whether some limit needs to be set. Unrestricted growth of the world population and unbridled growth of prosperity may well mean that one day there will be a price to pay. The crucial question is when the critical limit is reached and what factors affect this; resourceful management can shift this limit infinitely. However, these are forces that are currently not under our control. Perhaps new worldwide macro-organisational structures will be able to provide a solution (4, conclusion).

But once again, should human beings as absolute entities be happy with this? Or will such a development take place at the expense of other interests of absolute entities? Worse still, will it interfere to such an extent with one or more of the conditions for our existence that it must be slowed down or even stopped?

2 Inward-Looking (Closed), Goal in Itself (Autonomy, Being Yourself), Isolation and Communication (Broad and Immaterial)

Human beings as absolute entities are inward-looking, separate from all other absolute entities. We need to remember that all life forms are absolute entities and therefore all of them share this fate. Ordinarily, absolute entities can only observe the outside of another absolute entity, and cannot catch even the slightest glimpse of the inside. Body language is no exception. It can be considered an expression of something without revealing the underlying substrate of factors that play a role. More is required for this. Often, parts of it can be deduced from the circumstances, but it is still a matter of guesswork as to the actual causes of certain communications. A person's inner life and the deeper backgrounds always remain concealed for others as long they are not expressed in the commonly accepted manner.

This is one reason why human beings as absolute entities are on their own and can only seek their objectives within themselves. They are thus the goal in itself or in other words, autonomous in the sense of self. This autonomy must be distinguished from the fifth essential characteristic of absolute entities, or autonomy as self-determination. Both characteristics entail the third characteristic, which is that human beings as absolute entities live in isolation in an absolute sense, isolated from everything and everyone, even from their origins. Since they perceive this as very oppressive, they will do all they can to break out of their isolation. The obvious way to do so is by communicating using all possible means, in the broadest sense of the word. But because the state of isolation is absolute, it is in fact not possible to break out of it, and the means of communication are only ostensible possibilities and are therefore immaterial. The result is an imaginary connection. It exists only in the imagination of those involved. In addition, human beings can only communicate with limited and imperfect means, which leads to a great chance of misunderstanding or miscommunication. Recent developments in telephony and internet cannot alter this.

The most important general means of communication are those of language, involving signs (words, figures, symbols), images or sounds or a combination of these; they stimulate our senses and thus leave a certain impression in our brains. In everyday life, communication is usually incidental and fleeting. Words evaporate. Books, or at least texts, image and sound recordings give communication permanence. Certain forms of human behaviour (codes, manners, rituals) are intended to promote communication between people, although they may promote other objectives as well. We can thus regard religion and philosophy, art and culture, science and politics as forms of permanent communication between people.

3 Identity (Singularity, Character) and Individuality

We are living matter in a certain form, in which a number of specific characteristics are inherent, among them a number of unchanging hereditary traits that give us our own identity (singularity, character), by which we distinguish ourselves from other absolute entities (individuality).

Preamble (7)

Heredity might be described as passing on, by means of reproduction, factors that produce a resemblance of offspring to their parents. In a certain sense, every cell nucleus is an archive filled with documents, one that stores the complete list of hereditary factors of an organism. The documents are the chromosomes, which are present in all cells in equal numbers. Under the microscope they are visible as a jumble of short threadlike strands. Half of every chromosome pair comes from the father and half from the mother. Human beings have twenty-three pairs of chromosomes. In these macromolecules the genes (the carriers of the hereditary traits, genetic factors) are arranged like pearls on a chain, and each gene always occupies the same place in the chain.

We know that hereditary traits of our forebears recur over and over again in the family tree. The colour of our skin, eyes and hair is very clearly hereditary, as is the physique in a general sense (e.g. slender or stocky), and other hereditary traits to a lesser extent.

For a long time it was not known why the hereditary structure passed on from parent to child remained constant over many generations, even thousands of years. Biochemical research has shown that a complicated compound found almost exclusively in the cell nuclei of plants and animals forms the basis for life. This compound, deoxyribonucleic acid (DNA), is arranged in the form of an intertwined double helix with a multitude of crosslinks. Every cell nucleus forms an archive in which the chromosomes are the documents containing the construction diagram for the organism. These documents have number of chapters, the genes. When a cell divides, the construction diagram of the entire organism is passed on in the genetic code by means of complicated interaction.

Conclusion

Identity is the defining essential characteristic of human beings as absolute entities. It is this essential characteristic that makes people individuals. It is not shared a human trait as described in the other essential characteristics of people as absolute entities.

Their identity therefore reveals the innermost being of people, it touches the germ of life and thus is life itself. What makes it so special? We have learned that its characteristics can all be traced back to our material state of being, which includes certain substances that give us our own specific singularity. The field of genetics is a field that has not been fully explored (9). Quantum theory is still in its infancy (10). The conclusion nevertheless seems justified that further research might explain the riddles of life and might even allow us to break through into a subsequent dimension. But for the time being, we have reached a boundary.

4 Ultimate Objective: Self-Fulfilment (Development, Search for Meaning)

Self-fulfilment is achieved through self-development, i.e. discovering and honing our gifts and talents and thus finding our own identity (development), a process by which the lives of human beings as absolute entities acquire purpose (the search for meaning). Self-fulfilment is self-actualisation, the state that results from the realisation of the essential characteristics of human beings as absolute entities, and it leads to satisfaction derived from ourselves or our activities, a sense of being satisfied with what we have accomplished.

5 Autonomy (Self-Determination) and Freedom (Relative Freedom)

Autonomy means self-reliance, independence, the freedom to make your own choices, your own decisions about yourself, to the exclusion of others (self-determination), thus allowing you to actualise the essential characteristics of human beings as absolute entities. This freedom is relative in that it focuses on self-fulfilment, and so it is limited in this sense.

Experience (perception, cognisance)

This is the way in which human beings as absolute entities operate. Experience as a concept can be described as parts, or phases, of processes in the brain. These processes are autonomous. Accordingly, experience can be divided into the following parts or phases:

1 Observation (Input)
2 Storage (Memory)
3 Organising (Combining)
4 Conclusion or Finding (Mood, Intuition, Feelings, Emotions, Thought, Knowledge, Reason, Idea, Mental Grasp, Consciousness, Mind, Soul, Psyche, Will, Conscience, etc.)
5 Plan
6 Performance (Output)

1 Preamble (7)

All living organisms, even the simplest micro-organisms, are composed of cells. Despite differences in dimensions and form, all cells are essentially the same. The cell nucleus provides for the maintenance and reproduction of the living cell. Cells form new cells by dividing. The normal manner of cell division is called nuclear division. The formation of new DNA takes about eight hours, whereas nuclear division takes less than two hours. Human cells divide at most once a day; many types of cells divide only after weeks or months. In general, cell division is a brief, intense activity during a short period of the life of the cell, causing scarcely any interruption to its normal functioning.

The brain is part of the nervous system, containing all nerve centres that are needed to maintain life. They form the body's central checkpoint and make it possible for us to think, to plan and to experience. The nervous system has two basic functions: receiving and processing information and setting in motion and guiding movements for specific physical work. The central nervous system, to which the brain belongs, is the central exchange or checkpoint, coordinating and managing all life and bodily functions. Everything that we consciously feel or do starts in the central nervous system and is processed there. Our unconscious thoughts, feelings and conflicts can be found there as well.

Conclusion

Experience can thus be viewed as a process in the brain that is set in motion by stimuli to the senses. The information about this is stored and processed and, within fractions of seconds, is given a suitable reaction (by means of electrical impulses), apparently based on a situation or state that can best be qualified as a conclusion or finding, interpreted by us in terms of functions, such as mood, intuition, feelings, emotions, thought, ideas, wants or a property arising from these such as intellect, knowledge, conscience, mind, soul and psyche or a related state such as consciousness, the subconscious and the unconscious.

The process seems to take place autonomously and therefore to escape our observation and influence. This would mean that the phase in which the conclusion or finding is reached is a direct consequence of the data stored and processed in the brain cells. If this reasoning is correct, then the qualifications we use (mood, intuition, etc.) are inaccurate, misleading and confusing and they can better be replaced by the words conclusion or finding. After all, we are that process (5) and though appearances are deceiving thanks to the operation of the senses, what in fact takes place shows merely the distance within the process that we are still removed from reaching the phase of the conclusion, a matter of a fraction of a second.

We would be better off using the word conclusion or finding as our basis, at any rate to indicate the phase in which the process of experience finds itself. Both words refer to perception (immaterial) in contrast to experience (material). The words conclusion or finding do more justice to what takes place in this phase of the process of experience. The words we now use arouse the mistaken impression that there is another dimension outside of our empirical reality, which is not plausible.

2 The process of experience

How does the process of experience actually take place, and how can we explain the fact that we use so many different words for something that has to do with the same process?

To answer these questions, we must first of all realise that all these processes take place within fractions of seconds. Nerve impulses are transmitted at a speed of around fifty to one hundred metres per second. This makes it clear why a reaction time of approximately one second is necessary before a motorist recognises a danger and takes appropriate action, or when a person is holding his or her hand near a hot oven, before the muscles are told to withdraw the hand (7).

Viewed in this way, it seems reasonable that, depending on the complexity of the situation, the process of experience is longer or shorter. The more complex a situation, the more time it will take. A process of experience is autonomous, taking place outside of our field of observation and beyond our influence. This means that in complex situations we must wait longer for the conclusion or its implementation. This gives us a sense of uncertainty, which continues throughout the phase of ordering (combining) and lasts until the phase of the conclusion or finding, which is the only one that can provide us with certainty. Uncertainty means not knowing what to do or how to act. The scale from not-knowing to knowing is a sliding scale, i.e. the longer the phase of ordering and combining, the more knowledge we will gain, and each point in that process is accompanied by a different feeling, depending on the extent to which our not-knowing (uncertainty) has been converted into knowing (certainty).

In the first phase we are in the domain of mood, intuition, feeling, emotion and in the second phase the domain of thinking, ideas, intellect, reason and knowing. These are parts of one and the same ordering process which will lead to the conclusion or finding. Only the way we perceive it is translated into terms of feeling and knowing or not-knowing (5). We refer to the course of this process as unconscious and then move via the subconscious to consciousness; again, these are references to our perception and they are not actually correct because the process of experience continues without interruption, although outside of our field of observation and beyond our influence, and therefore autonomously; because we are these processes of experience (5), they take place within ourselves; we are one with them, indivisibly linked.

3 Dreams, visions, paranormal phenomena, ghosts and apparitions Meditation

But then how can we explain dreams, visions and paranormal phenomena (clairvoyance, clairsentience and clairaudience), ghosts and apparitions? And what exactly is meditation?

In medical terms, dreams are sometimes defined as the fantasies, thoughts and other mental activities that occur while we are asleep. From this we may conclude that the process of experience continues without interruption, not only in our waking state but in sleep as well, and that it is thus an autonomous process, outside our field of observation and beyond our influence. The images in our dreams are simply a result of the empirical visual observation that took place in a waking state, the stimuli of which (visual, photographic) have been stored (set down) in the brain cells and the images of which can become visible during sleep.

Taking this one step further, some people have visions; they see paranormal phenomena, ghosts and apparitions, which also result in images or visions that arise in the same way, though here they are not limited to sleep, but are also seen in a waking state.

The shared characteristic of all these phenomena is that the images can manifest themselves in present, past or future (multidimensional, broader, deeper). From this it might be concluded that the time-space dimension is absent, or in other words, that the images thus evoked are not limited by time or space but can be approached directly in their state of being, where many interconnections can be viewed.

Meditating is generally defined as looking inward to experience the deepest reality, meditation as an attempt to experience the deepest reality by means of internal contemplation and transcendental meditation as meditation intended to separate the mind from the body. Meditating means being one and the same (11), your deepest (cosmic) state of being, by separating yourself from empirical reality (the process of experience) and looking inward in your own self as an absolute entity, which is part of your origins (evolution and history) with which you as an entity are linked. During the process, your essential characteristics are aligned with your most original state of being, thus bringing about a state of equilibrium (peace).

From this we may conclude that the former phenomena and meditation are not the same, but quite the opposite. The former arise from the process of experience and empirical reality and are part of it, while meditation can be viewed as an attempt to withdraw from reality and its sphere of influence, and so is not part of it.

4 Multiplicity of processes
Sliding scale

Experience is not just a single process, but a multitude of them throughout one's entire life. It leads to what we call a person, or a mind, a soul, a psyche, a totality of experiences, which gradually cause someone to exhibit certain personal characteristics related to his or her own identity (singularity, character), to that by which he or she distinguishes himself from others (individuality). We now want to look at what happens on that sliding scale from not-knowing to knowing, the process which we need so many words to describe, even though it is all part of the same process. In the first phase of this process (not-knowing) we are in the domain of feelings and emotions, and in the second phase in the domain of knowing, where feelings have been converted into knowing. And remember, all this takes place in just a fraction of a second.

5 The meaning of the words we use (8)(38)

Because the meaning of words is so important, we will first define them and then see what happens and how:

Mood
1 emotional tone that accompanies human beings in their continual activity
2 all-embracing and lasting emotional state (in contrast to affect)
Intuition
form of understanding not based on reasoning, experience or knowing

Feelings
becoming innerly aware, perceiving
Emotions
feelings that are consciously observed, in contrast to affect, which is about both conscious feelings and urges
Affect
brief but vehement emotion

Thought
inner processing and treatment of data from observation or from the memory
Knowledge
capacity to think and to understand
Reason
capacity of human beings to render an account of the world and themselves, to know grounds and arguments and to act accordingly; see also sense
Sense
sense (good sense, common sense), wits
Idea
representation existing in the mind, concept, thought
Mental Grasp
the whole of meaning, experience, general concepts and statements
Knowing
Understanding
Understanding
having knowledge of

Consciousness
1. sensory state in which people efficiently process and/or respond to stimuli from the outside world and from their own body, and in which they are aware that their body is functioning
2. arriving at a certain awareness through thought

Subconscious (psychology, psychiatry)
1. the portion of what people have forgotten that is trying to return to their consciousness and that thus exerts an influence on their behaviour
2. in psychoanalytic theory: level of consciousness between unconscious and conscious

Unconscious
the whole of processes that influence behaviour, but that are not apparent to our consciousness

Person
independently acting human being, individual
Mind
a number of functions of the body: thinking, feeling and wanting
Soul
mind or psyche
Psyche
total of conscious and unconscious inner experiences of an individual organism, soul, mind

Will
the human capacity to strive for something

Conscience
learned awareness of good and evil, moral consciousness.

6 Billions of cell bodies
Structural, functional and incidental information

Our body consists of a single large mass of cells (living matter) that possess a treasure of information that we are unable to grasp, and that, depending on the place where those cells are located, make us do everyday things. The nature of this information might perhaps be classified into structural (DNA, chromosomes, genes), functional (hunger, thirst, fatigue, sexual feelings, etc.) and incidental (related to the process of experience). The incidental source of information is situated in the brain, which can be regarded as the coordination centre. The management of all life and bodily functions is conducted in the brain, and it is here that what we call conscious or unconscious feelings, thoughts, plans, conflicts, etc. are found (7).

All brain activity can be regarded as an autonomous process that escapes our observation and is beyond our influence; it is entirely managed by our structural, functional and incidental antennas. This process continues when we are asleep and even when we are unconscious. Our dreams confirm this. When we wake up and open our eyes, our incidental information provision goes on without flagging, whether we like it or not. What we do at that point might be described as entering the train that is our process of experience and becoming entirely absorbed by it. When we rouse ourselves from sleep, wash and dress, have breakfast, it may seem to be a conscious experience, but in fact we are simply being guided by our cells; an extra dimension of consciousness has nothing to do with it.

In our sleeping state we are not conscious of ourselves, but our empirical processes of experience (except for observation and storage of new sensory stimuli) continue nevertheless. In our waking state we are fully taken up by the process of experience, and as an entity, a oneness, we are part of it. We are the process of experience (5). The unconscious cannot alter the way our process of experience moves forward. We may or may not be involved (to a limited extent) in the process of experience. If we see a tree, we are not conscious of that tree, but we are in an uninterrupted flow from our eyes to the tree, which we observe via our brain cells. Here the word consciousness is not appropriate; what we are involved in is merely an empirical experiment, namely the course of the process of observation. And the same applies to what we call feeling, thinking and wanting. If we referred to these as experiencing, it would do more justice to what actually happens. The words we use arouse the suggestion of a non-existent human dimension.

The concepts of person, mind, soul and psyche give the overall picture of all the characteristics that we possess, that we can observe in ourselves and in others and that are connected to our experience in relation to our origin and evolution and our essential characteristics as absolute entities. In fact the same objections are attached to the use of such words as those described above in relation to consciousness, feeling, thinking and wanting. This applies all the more to the emotionally charged word soul and to a somewhat lesser extent to the word mind. It is therefore preferable in my opinion to replace these words by a different word - characteristics, for example - because this word does more justice to what actually takes place.

7 Conscience and the Other
Conflict of interests

The experience of our conscience belongs in the same category as feeling, thinking and wanting. However, it has a special aspect, namely the presence of other human beings as absolute entities. Generally speaking, the process of experience is concerned with the way to best promote your own interests, with how far you will go in actualising your essential characteristics as an absolute entity. The discussion of our urge for survival showed that we can go quite far in that respect, and that to actualise that urge, there are in fact no boundaries; everything is permitted.

The same can be said about actualising our other essential characteristics, but the difference is that our need to do so is perhaps less cogently present; it is not our life, or at least not our continued material existence, that is at stake. Nonetheless, we can and may even choose to go to extremes in this respect and thus to give ourselves priority over others.

This leaves two possibilities: either it brings you into conflict with the other, or you step back of your own accord, perhaps after a showdown with another person, and decide simply to make the best of it. You can drive a conflict so high that you go to extremes, even death. You can also come to your senses and decide to step back. Finally, you can decide in advance that you do not want to let things come to this juncture for any reason at all, and pull back.

These possibilities share at least one common characteristic: they are all related to the presence of the other; the interest of another person is at stake, giving rise to the question of how you will deal with it. If you give your own interests priority at the expense of the other, it is good for you, but you as an absolute entity have surely experienced what this means for the other; in a fleeting moment, it has presented itself. You can go on like this endlessly, but at some point, perhaps not until the end of your life, you will realise what it means to another person when you realise what it means to you when it happens to you. This may well constitute a reason to change your behaviour towards others. The reason to respect the other person's interests is therefore found only in the fact that you do not want to have such an experience yourself; it is not found in the interests of the other person. This experience or this awareness can lead you to take it into account in your behaviour at an early stage and to encourage the same thing in others. This is what we call the conscience. From this point of view, good means good for yourself and therefore for others as well. You realise that when you injure another person, you primarily harm yourself. If you do not, many people will regard you as an unprincipled reprobate and you will feel the consequences.

Respect for the interests of others is therefore based on self-respect, which may lead you to decide to subject your dealings with other people to a set of standards for yourself. Here we enter the area of morals and ethics, to which we can attach a complete moral philosophy and on the basis of a belief, a moral theology. At the end of this road is total love of yourself and others, because you have come to realise that it is the only way that can lead to the fourth essential characteristic of human beings as absolute entities, namely self-fulfilment. You will then have developed in a way that allows you to give yourself and others the scope we need as absolute entities (compassion, solidarity).

Summary

To summarise, human beings as absolute entities have undergone developments over millions of years (they have evolved) so that today we can point to a number of traits (essential characteristics) in connection with their nature and origin, which we have looked at from a point of view that we generally call empirical reality (the process of experience). In this process our empirical involvement can be regarded as the motor that has made us, or caused us to develop, into what we are today. This is our everyday reality. This alone has given us our essential characteristics (urge for survival, communication, identity, self-fulfilment, self-determination), and these essential characteristics can be seen as the motives - which have proved in the course of history to be enduring - for our actions. This implies that they do not truly exist, but they apparently typify our most original state of being, set down in billions of cells (matter) that make us who we are.

It follows from the nature of human beings as absolute entities that the way in which they get along with each other is primarily determined by the free interplay of forces. They can impose limitations (self-limitations, voluntarily) on themselves for the sake of peace (conscience) and can avail themselves of norms (rules of morals and decency) as guidelines for their actions. This involves the relationships between individuals in contrast to individuals in a group (family and friends, clubs, companies, religious communities, government) where the group imposes norms (rules of morals and decency, mores, customs and usages, laws) on its participants, who must adhere to them.

We can thus conclude that the free interplay of forces (absolute freedom) is inherent in human nature, that any limitation of this is alien to human nature and that the use of norms is only prompted by a need for ordering, depending on the circumstances (efficiency), when there is a clash of interests. This absolute freedom in connection with the realisation of the total of all essential characteristics of human beings as absolute entities in relation to others must be distinguished from the relative freedom of people in realising their autonomy in the form of self-determination, which is limited in this sense.

IV Description

Definition of experience

In the course of history, the term experience has been used in so many different senses that at the very least this can be said to have led to some confusion as to what it actually means (12). In the sense I use, the term refers only to the process of experience as parts (phases) of processes in the brain that take place autonomously, beyond our field of observation and without us being able to exert any influence on them.

We are therefore ourselves the process of experience (5), meaning that an uninterrupted whole of processes takes place, controlled by our structural, functional and incidental antennas. All these processes are focused on achieving the objectives and promoting the ensuing interests that are peculiar to each human being as an absolute entity and that are anchored in him or her, are irrevocably bound up with her or him.

From this it follows that the development of human beings as absolute entities is an automatic process that takes place of its own accord; we do not need to do anything in particular for it. The feelings, thoughts, ideas, levels of consciousness, etc. that we derive from this are our interpretation of what takes place, but do not actually exist (5). This dualistic approach to the process of experience is understandable from the human perspective, but it is not in line with the facts. This may explain the confusion about the meaning of the term experience; its meaning must first be clarified and hopefully, consensus achieved in this respect before we can develop further ideas on that basis as to the nature of human beings and their origin and evolution. This meaning of the term experience is derived chiefly from an interior focus, an introspective approach to human beings; it is on this basis that the world in which human beings live can be explained. This perspective is crucial if we are to arrive at a proper understanding of things and avoid further confusion.

The problem thus outlined is primarily due to the fact that we do not regard experience as one and the same process of experience which is us, the parts (phases) of which are inextricably bound up with each other, but which are separate from each other, meaning that our sensory observation, thoughts, consciousness and actions are all ascribed independent meaning. When we isolate sensory observation from the rest, our attention is automatically focused on the outside world (exterior), and thought (reason, mental grasp, a priori ideas), feelings and consciousness are then situated in several places somewhere in the brain (13); on this basis the world is explained without any reference to the origin and evolution of human beings, to their very essence. This same perspective allows us to explain the seeming antithesis between empiricism and rationalism.

Because an independent location and meaning is attributed to all these terms, we lose sight of the fact that they are all derived from the dualistic and non-existent human dimension and are thus not based on the unity of the process of experience in the brain - which has been scientifically proven - consisting of related and dependent parts (phases). This explains why certain issues in relation to the world around us have still not been resolved even after centuries of study; they can only be resolved if we include the possibility of a unified process of experience in our considerations. Only from that point of view does it become possible to view the world (nature) as something with which human beings as absolute entities are in a state of continual exchange, from which they arise and of which they are part, as are all life forms as well as inanimate nature.

Objectives and interests
Motives

These terms are used here in a specific sense. In this context, the interests of human beings as absolute entities are fully determined by the objectives that are inherent in our essence. We refer to the reasons why we promote our interests arising from this as our motives (driving force, energy) for actualising our objectives. So our purposes and our interests are points on the same line and can be regarded as the whole of objectives and interests (in a broad sense, i.e. everything that can contribute to the attainment of our objectives). The sphere of influence in which people are always entangled for the attainment of their objectives often obscures or veils the type of promotion of interests or the concrete objective. This is because of the nature of the process of experience, which is autonomous; it takes place beyond our field of observation and we can exert no influence on it.

Theoretically, we might say that everything felt to be useful to the realisation of our objectives may be qualified as an interest, and promoting our interests can help us to achieve them. However, as this is not always clear, it can often only be assessed in retrospect. In everyday life people often are not aware of the objectives they are working to achieve. They are guided by their structural, functional and incidental antennas, which give them a broad general sense that they should go in a certain direction, without actually knowing where they are going, rather like a compass. So we tend to feel that we are walking in a maze, one in which we can only determine our course on the basis of our own personal compass, the process of experience. This is how people go through life; it is structurally determined and in principle it always applies.

Of course this does not detract from the fact that during their lives people do build up some form of expertise, of which, after time, they form some idea. We can learn a great many lessons from the course of human history. But although time and place and circumstances are factors that are continually subject to change, the basis always remains the same. Thanks to our experiential history, we are now reasonably able to establish with some certainty (33)(44) the nature of human beings and their origin and evolution. This means that we should probably be able to expose a cross-section of human life by going in somewhat greater depth into our objectives, the interests they represent and the motives related to them. If we can achieve greater clarity in this respect, then we will also be better able to understand the behaviour of human beings as absolute entities and to attach consequences to it.

The relationship of the process of experience to our origin and evolution and our essential characteristics
The world of human beings as absolute entities

The starting point is always the process of experience of which human beings are part in everyday life. However you look at it, this is always the basis. It is where everything converges: our origin and evolution and our essential characteristics that do not really exist, but that can be seen as motives for action anchored in an absolute sense in each person's being. And then the only possible conclusion is that our objectives lie along this same line and can be formulated as a corollary to our origin and evolution and our essential characteristics: they arise directly from them and are related to them. Since these aspects are all intertwined in everyday life, the distinctions we make are not adequate to describe them. A cross-section must be made so as to expose a large number of cross-connections. This means that we will explain the distinctions we have made, separate them and then classify them in a logical relationship to one another.

1 Reproduction

In this connection we must first of all discuss the objective related to the urge to procreate or in other words, to beget progeny. This objective is not classified with the essential characteristics of human beings because although it can be regarded as a decisive aspect of life (14), its consequences do not serve any immediate objective in our lives as absolute entities; in itself, it does not make any changes to our objectives, but at most it provides for progeny, new life, which in its turn (from the time of birth) bears in it the characteristics of human beings as absolute entities and can take part in the cyclic process of reproduction. So this aspect can solely be regarded as part of our origin and evolution, from which people as absolute entities have emerged. The fact that our reproductive urge can be regarded as all-controlling does not require any explanation; this is related to its location in segments that are part of our human origin and evolution which stand in a hierarchical relationship, so that the influences of the first three segments (cosmos, nature and man) make themselves felt, with which human beings are in a constant state of interaction. It will be clear that the process of experience is interwoven with this and that it is a major motive driving people together, meaning that they will always be involved with each other.

2 Survival

The main objective of human beings as absolute entities is related to our urge for survival, because in a material sense we are not self-supporting, but completely dependent on what nature offers us. In earlier times survival instincts meant that we lived as hunters, guided by our functional antennas. Today, this activity can be described as economically motivated, basically including everything that can be assumed to be serviceable, so it must therefore be construed very broadly - not merely providing in our primary needs, but everything else that is necessary for this. As our human society becomes more complex and more prosperous, secondary activities to attain the primary necessities of life become more comprehensive. In our present day and age they are even so multi-faceted that we can now expect to be occupied with such activity for perhaps the greatest part of our life, possibly even without being truly aware of it on a daily basis.

After all, the sole objective of technological developments, both past and present (innovation), is economic. They brought the first major changes to our human society, so that we could produce more goods more quickly, and people have had to adapt considerably to these changes. Producing more implies consuming more. For several reasons, a government became necessary, one which could impose a minimum of order on society. The necessary infrastructure was developed. Business organisations and government banded together to ensure a good balance in working conditions (in a broad sense). Healthcare was organised and a wide range of educational facilities put in place. And to ensure that everything went well, social provisions were established such as the armed forces, the fire brigade, the police and the judicial authorities. These are all essentially secondary aspects that have been created to facilitate economic life, with the ultimate goal of maximising opportunities for the survival of one and all; all of them are thus interests that can be helpful in this respect and they serve as incentives to motivate human beings as absolute entities.

Although we often seem to forget this in our everyday life, we must realise that our great prosperity in today's world is something that came about thanks to our joint efforts. And from this it can be deduced that the role reserved for government is one of complete servitude to economic life, a role so important that not only do we expect government to facilitate the economy, but under certain circumstances even to participate in it when the interests of society at large are at stake (creating jobs in recessions, energy supply, traffic provisions etc.). Ordinarily, however, the role of the government is more in the background, limited to creating frameworks and facilities without actually taking part in society and the lives of citizens. On the other hand, in that same context we can well imagine that we may have gone overboard in our adulation of economic development. We have long since passed the critical point that marks the boundary between survival and waste, and are even seeing many side effects affecting the environment and our search for meaning (spirituality), meaning that we are drifting, which is always a risky business, and are now in urgent need of a counter-movement to help restore an equilibrium.

It is hugely important to be aware that most activities of human beings as absolute entities, whether they are acting as individuals, members of society or citizens, either directly or indirectly involve an economic motive. The meaning behind our activities thus generally has an economic background and we borrow this knowledge from the reasoning we have followed, starting from human beings as absolute entities with their origin and evolution and essential characteristics; in this case their urge for survival is decisive. Without this starting point it will be well-nigh impossible to define the meaning and deeper backgrounds of what motivates people in their daily lives. This implies that, in itself, the political, social and cultural life of human beings cannot help us discover our underlying motives; we can only learn this by reflecting on our origin and evolution and essential characteristics, which can be considered enduring motives for our actions.

3 Communication
The world of the imagination

Only when human beings have finally managed to ensure their survival can they deal with the objective related to their second essential characteristic, the fact that they live in isolation, from which they try to escape by communicating for reasons other than economic, using all the means available to them. In contrast to the first essential characteristic (the urge for survival), which is of a material nature, communication, as we have seen, is of an immaterial nature, related to the impossibility of breaking out of our physical (closed, inward-looking) isolation, which means that communication does not actually exist, but is imaginary (fictitious). This is the world of the imagination (15), where everything is possible.

Again, our starting point is the everyday world of human beings as absolute entities, which is simply the process of experience. Large-scale contradictions and seeming inconsistencies play a role in this world - on the one hand, the concrete circumstances in which you are brought into this world (thanks to the cyclic process), and on the other hand, remaining constantly alert to the forces involved in reproduction and survival. As if that were not enough, the non-existent world of the imagination is woven into this: our dreams and fantasies, which urge themselves upon us automatically thanks to our inward-looking nature. This is an extremely confusing, frightening and uncertain state (isolation), in which every one of us must find our own way (develop) in the search for our own identity (individuality), always with the final objective of fulfilling our own essence (the search for meaning). As we have seen, our journey is guided automatically by the process of experience, in which all these elements come together, so that we need only to follow our own compass. In this context the significance of our essential characteristic of autonomy in the form of self-determination lies not so much in our decisions, which would imply taking responsibility. It sooner takes the form of a claim on others; it is more the desire to be left to your own devices (as a being unto yourself, an acceptance of who you are) by others, thus shaping the relative freedom of human beings as absolute entities.

In simple terms, communication is an attempt to connect (to make an imaginary connection) with another human being. However, a great deal can go wrong, resulting in miscommunication or misunderstandings. In everyday dealings this takes place (incidentally, fleetingly) in our direct contacts with other persons, against a background of economic or simply social reasons (exchange of information in a broad sense, networking). In relation to the second essential characteristic of human beings as absolute entities, we mean communication undertaken for other reasons, which can therefore take place in all other fields in which people are active. Typical of this type of communication is that the content of the message is considerably more complex; direct contact is inadequate for its transfer, so that some other means (indirect, with a permanent form) must be sought, thus giving communication a permanence in our lives. We have seen that texts, textbooks, image and sound recordings are means of permanent communication and that religion and philosophy, art and culture, science and politics are expressions of this and therefore also belong to the world of the imagination (15).

The most important characteristic of communication, whether in its permanent form or not, is that it is based on the closed, inward-looking isolation in which people find themselves and from which they are continually trying to escape. Here lies the strength of every human creation, the extent to which and the manner in which this aspect of the lives of human beings is intertwined with the work they have created. Every one of us follows our own path in this respect, and we try to involve others with us in a way that is compelling, inspiring. From this great creations are born, the subjects of which may lie in all fields in which people are active, or which cause them concern or pleasure, leading to a sense of appreciation. The undertone can vary from extremely serious to light-hearted and casual, depending on the subject in which people recognise themselves, and evoking the entire gamut of feelings and thoughts of human beings. We must not forget that these are all typically human approaches to our human qualities, that they are the only means available to us, and even what we produce in our wildest dreams cannot obscure the fact that what we are involved in is all imagination, which is therefore simply our own personal reality or truth and which has nothing to do with any so-called absolute truth in which people would so gladly believe, but which would immediately destroy this sphere of influence and fully disregard our empirical involvement.

Eight billion people as absolute entities

The way I have described human beings as absolute entities in their origins, their essence and their mode of operation is the status that all share equally, which also indicates how they relate and are related. They all manifest themselves on the basis of their own empirical reality, on the basis of their own process of experience. The process of experience in operation is the here and now. I will restrict myself to this because it cannot be said to include the past and the future. We can no longer influence the past and what we know of it comes from hearsay and history books; we would do well to ask ourselves whether the picture they sketch faithfully reflects reality, and even if it does, whether we receive the picture as it was intended, or moulded on our own vague conjectures.

After all, we can establish facts, but we are unable to get to the bottom of the entire breadth of the evolution and history on which they are based. From our situation in the here and now, we try to form a picture of this but it is completely coloured by the process of experience peculiar to us at this time; the longer ago the history and the more remote the past, the more this is the case. We know significantly less about the Greeks and the Romans, the Jews and the Christians than we do about World War I and II. As history becomes more ancient, images become vague, and we tend to fill in missing bits, thus distorting them by our own colourations. Every phase in history is to this extent unique (a one-time event); it is bygone, over, done with, finished. The influence of history on our picture of the present - not to mention the future - is therefore of limited significance. It is one more reason not to pay attention to the time-space dimension, but to restrict ourselves to our state of being.

And so we limit ourselves to today's world, in which eight billion people are all trying to find their own way. Only two aspects are important here: the way in which each of them does this individually, and their mutual relations. Furthermore, each of them has his or her own empirical reality, their own truth. This consists of billions of cells that are continually being replaced and that provide us with structural, functional and incidental information. The information flows can be regarded as processes that allow us to act in accordance with their content. They are autonomous processes that take place beyond our field of observation and on which we are unable to exert any influence.

The information structurally present in our cells is passed on to our descendants. The functional information (hunger, thirst, fatigue, sex etc.) is autonomously passed on to our brain cells, which let us do what is necessary to satisfy our perceived needs (incidental information). Our entire essence is permeated by this. It describes how our first essential characteristic develops within us, how our urge for survival obviates our dependence. The greatest part of our lives is taken up by this - providing in the first necessities of life, directly or indirectly. And in our present day and age we may say that this takes up almost our whole life (materialism) and that we are doing our utmost to involve the entire world (globalisation), something which is not without consequences (the environment, the search for meaning). Survival is not the same thing as bathing in luxury (waste), which is what we are doing now.

Sooner or later each person is confronted with the question: why? What is the deeper background to this? What is the meaning, what is the point? Exactly what are we doing? And in a somewhat broader context, what is the point of life? Is there a God and a life after this one, or is life the one we know now, no more and no less? These are questions people of all ages have asked themselves - and we have been able to establish that none of them can be answered. In the past, people had their own definitions for this, depending on time, place and circumstances. But by now we should know better. The deeper significance of life will always remain a riddle.

V Application

The playing field of illusion
Disillusion

1 Communication

We have seen that people are isolated and as a result, they do all they can to break out of it. This is done by communication using all possible means (in a broad sense). But we have also seen that the forms of communication available to us offer only spurious possibilities (immaterial) because it is not physically possible to break out of our isolation. We can only make an imaginary connection to those outside of ourselves. People who communicate imagine that they are in contact with one another. They do this by making use of language, images or sounds or a combination of these, or by certain forms of behaviour. We have also seen that communication is mostly fleeting and that communication can take on a more permanent form in texts, books, image and sound recordings. Lastly, we have seen that religion and philosophy, art and culture, science and politics are all permanent forms of communication.

From this it follows that communication does not truly exist; it is illusory. Communication cannot alter our isolation. Means of communication are expressions of what people experience, of the process of experience that they perceive and of which they are part, that they are themselves (5). They take place outside the introversion, the inward-looking world of people in a sort of space that we could term the playing field of illusion: there the exchange takes place, there the connection is made.

We must also make a distinction between forms of communication (the means) and the content of the message they put across. As we have seen, communication entails a fair chance of misunderstanding or miscommunication. This means that, to actually put a message across, the sender must have a clear idea of its contents. The sender must correctly translate the contents of the message into the means of communication of choice, so that the recipient of the message can reasonably be expected to understand it (in an objective sense). The recipient will receive the message via his or her own process of experience, thus colouring the translation, which is now different from the original intention of the sender. The original intention of the sender can be approached more closely by conducting further or more intensive communication until both sender and recipient have the impression that the communication properly reflects the intention.

Communication takes place in phases: it starts in the first phase, the process of experience in the sender, moving via the playing field of illusion, to end in the final phase of the process of experience in the recipient. This information flow comprises no end of opportunities that could lead to misunderstanding or miscommunication. The social skills and intelligence of those who take part play a big role in this respect. We can thus ascertain that we are dealing with a complicated process in which there is but a slight chance that the contents of the message will be identical for both sender and recipient.

In everyday life it is often about simple things, things that tend to find their own way. In economic issues (focused on survival) matters become a bit more complicated. Just think how long it took before mankind arrived at the first forms of capitalism, division of labour and specialisation, not to mention enterprise-based production. In the other fields that have to do with communication (from religion to politics) - extremely complicated matters - communication is not possible unless it is given permanence. This means we are dealing with thought processes that are not only extremely complex, but that are also lengthy and require much time. The most important issues for people are then dealt with first, such as religion and philosophy, but just think how long it has taken us to arrive at the religions as we know them in today's world, or at least what is left of them (34).

For all these areas in the field of communication, the less permanent the communication, the poorer will be the results. In many fields we must rely on books, or bits of them, that tell us very little about the ideas of the past. We know less about the philosophers than we do of the Roman Catholic Church, which has an Old and a New Testament, church buildings, rituals and language, a worldwide organisation with a hierarchical power structure and not to be forgotten, doctrines to which people are held accountable. The scope of this power institution indicates the importance that large portions of the world population apparently wish to attach to religion.

From an even later date are organised science and politics. There too, people have indicated the importance they attach to them. Most true sciences have in fact only been around since the previous century. Present political life in the most powerful countries of the world is the result of the Enlightenment, which took place in the eighteenth century, moving from England and America towards Europe. Mankind clearly needed a great deal of time to devise and implement democracy in its present form. You might say that the solidity of Western democracies reflects their permanence, so that even religious power institutions have become subordinate to them.

But this does not always mean that the more permanence a means of communication has, the more brilliant are the ideas it is intended to portray. Permanence is often a matter of navigating in an unsteady balance while struggling to survive. In that sense the chances for religious power institutions (hierarchical and religious) are greater than for political organisations (democratic and economic). The ideas on which they are based may have been thought up and communicated by people, but were nonetheless derived from the playing field of illusion, so they do not really exist. One might say that as permanence increases, the original idea is at a farther remove and less is left of its authenticity because all manner of irrelevant aspects that are alien to it have been incorporated. In this sense, within the power institution of the Roman Catholic Church, very little remains of the original Christian ideals that motivated people. We might well say that the modern democratic states under the rule of law have hollowed out the original idea of freedom to a not inconsiderable degree. The ideas of the philosophers, artists and intellectuals, in so far as they were not under the command of the Church or the State, have remained preserved in the most authentic (original, real) form and therefore appeal more to the imagination.

2 Free exchange of Ideas

The free exchange of ideas (communication) on the playing field of illusion thus provides in a fundamental necessity of life of people and can inspire people. In principle, it makes no difference what a person thinks or says, as long as you think and say what you think to take part in the game of illusion. In fact this observation means that there can be no such thing as an objective, absolute truth. No-one in the world will ever be able to claim that they own the truth. On the playing field of illusion, truth simply does not exist. Everyone can therefore at most have his or her own reality, and share it with another person, to then observe that it is only relative, being dependent on time, place and circumstances.

The principle stated here lies at the basis of the democratic constitutional state and is entirely counter to the closed system as used by the Roman Catholic Church. This global church pretends that it owns the absolute truth and has worked out the idea on which this is based, the Holy Trinity consisting of God the Father, the Son and the Holy Spirit, in the form of dogmas and rules to rule people's entire lives. The mother church is located in Vatican City, a city-state in Rome that maintains diplomatic and other relations with all countries of the world, and therefore has its own organisational structure and legislation complete with sanctions for non-compliance. At its head is the Pope, who even today rules as an absolute monarch over his domain with a completely hierarchical structure, in which all others are subordinate to him. This church also pretends to be the keeper of the original Christian ideals.

The origin of (Judeo-) Christian ideals can be found in the Old and the New Testament; these, the oldest permanent forms of Christian communication, endure yet today and Christians, particularly Protestants, draw inspiration from them. The Roman Catholic Church has imposed a number of rules on this which it translates into everyday reality and makes known to the world community as its standpoint in the form of encyclicals. It also utilises numerous other forms of communication, such as the media (its own and those of others), churches, robes, rituals, language, music, aid organisations, pastoral services, missionary work, cloisters, etc. The faithful are subjected to rules that control nearly their entire lives, with a great many associated procedures and sanctions. In brief, it is an all-dominant organisation.

You might say that the Roman Catholic Church has made full use of the means of communication available to it. Of course this is beneficial for its permanence, and the world has a Christian culture that has been in existence for centuries, but one may also ask what is in fact left in daily life of the original Christian ideals, leaving to one side the question of the amount of truth in the basic idea to which the faithful commit themselves. It should be remembered that the absolute power of the Church and the Pope is based on this, as if this faith is no longer a faith, but simply the presumed absolute truth. Here the power institution stands in contrast to the loving community of Jesus Christ, who often seems farther away than ever.

Because of the extensive organisation and elaboration of the former, the latter comes under great pressure. Whether God exists is an important question, but debate on this must continue to be inspiring, not a battle lost before it begins. There must be room for doubt and for this reason no justification can ever be found for the creation of such a power institution, which ought to be reduced to loving (human) proportions by making modest use of the means of communication appropriate to this, not means of power that only interfere with the illusion and turn it into disillusion, throwing people back onto their isolation.

But moderation is a virtue, and the result is that the matters that have been added and incorporated take on independent meaning, apart from the meaning of the original idea. This is not to say that all Christian cultural communications are without meaning; quite the contrary, I would almost say, but even so, a bit more restraint would certainly be better. It is primarily the characteristics by which the power institution makes itself known, hierarchy, doctrines and rules with sanctions, that could do with some tinkering; this would give the Church a more human face and would reinstate the connection with the original Christian ideals. The Roman Catholic Church would then be able to become accessible (once again) for everyone, believer or non-believer, because it would then enter the playing field of illusion and would no longer stand on the sidelines.

The caricature of power

1 Voluntariness and involuntariness

Any way in which power is exercised that is in conflict with the interests, or against the will of other people (it is done without their consent) makes a caricature of that person's power or the person who wields it. Such exercise of power is contrary to the nature of human beings as absolute entities and therefore contrary to their being and their essential characteristics. Generally speaking, the use of power can be regarded as a form of promotion of interests, and not much objection can be made to this. If people's activities are economically motivated (survival), then the power exercised in that context is generally permissible. This changes when we enter the field of communication (the playing field of illusion) and the economic motive does not play a role. This is primarily the case in permanent forms of communication (religion and philosophy, art and culture, science and politics), all of which take place on the playing field of illusion, where no-one can claim that their truth is absolute nor can they expect another person to recognise it as such.

Specifically, being in a position of power and wielding power have an effect on our relationships with other people, in which there is a role for morals and ethics. It is always a matter between individuals, each of whom work in their own way to promote their own interests. But when they are unable to promote certain of their interests on their own, they will band together, something that takes place in all fields imaginable. When they take this step, human beings as absolute entities step outside of themselves, thus shaping a form of co-existence the nature of which can be both material and immaterial: immaterial because they are driven together by a shared motive, and material when, as a group, they give shape to their collaboration by setting up a range of social institutions. This manner of promoting individual and collective interests knows no bounds, and will always result in the unlimited pursuit of their own interests and the related unbridled exercise of power, which inevitably leads to all manner of social problems. Moreover, it implies an incessant struggle (between individuals) and war (between groups), things people commonly engage in yet today.

People only recently came to understand this, and they developed the concept of a democratic constitutional state, which created a basis for them to live together peacefully. The chief characteristic of a constitutional democracy is that people subject themselves to its regime voluntarily, thus legitimating the power it holds as well as its exercise. But there are limits to anything to which people voluntarily subject themselves, and the objectives of a constitutional democracy must largely be in line with promotion of the individual and collective interests of its subjects, on whose support the constitutional democracy must be able to rely. And as we have seen, the focus of their interests will primarily be economic (i.e. survival).

Democracy can thus exert its influence on society as a whole as well as on the individual citizens, and the longer its period of development (thus having attained a higher degree of organisation), the more will its influence be felt. The immaterial concept of the constitutional democracy has taken shape in the form of material democratic institutions that are anchored in society. Thanks to the present high organisational level of most Western democracies, nearly all social institutions are amply legitimated and derive their identity from this, allowing them to share some of the state's power and endowing them with certain competencies or powers to act to the exclusion of others. Despite the fact that citizens and societal institutions enjoy a large degree of freedom to act as they see fit, government has gained a considerable grip on society as a whole. As a result, it has been able to set limits to competition and rivalry and to power and its exercise (cartels, monopolies, etc.) by means of legislation, and to exact compliance, if necessary with the use of force.

Beyond the scope of economic life, and especially on the playing field of illusion (permanent forms of communication), government influence should be kept to a minimum because this is the exclusive domain of individual citizens. It should be reserved to them because it is where they can bring to expression their essential characteristics as absolute entities (communication, identity, the search for meaning, autonomy), areas in which they ought to be entirely free. These essential characteristics have therefore acquired an important place within a constitutional democracy in the form of basic rights and freedoms that protect citizens against the power of the state (freedom of opinion, of association and meeting, mental and physical integrity, religion etc.). In fact the role of the government can largely be defined as creating the frameworks in which individual citizens can move freely (or as freely as possible).

3 Religion and religiosity
The Roman Catholic Church

Religiosity (in a broad sense, spirituality, mysticism, etc.) of human beings as absolute entities is a matter that takes place on the playing field of the illusion and should therefore be regarded as strictly personal. If people turn their religious feelings into a religion (in a narrow sense), then we may speak of permanence in their communication, set down in books, in which its evolution and history and meaning are described, thus providing it with a certain legitimacy as a religion. Some religions go even further in this respect by creating a wide range of societal institutions such as churches and organisations that provide social services (in a broad sense), so as to anchor themselves in society.

If a religion then attaches to its evolution and history and its meaning a complex of rules to live by, it enters the terrain of morals and ethics, in which people voluntarily apply norms in their interpersonal dealings, norms they have devised themselves and for which they hold themselves personally responsible. In religions, these rules to live by are generally devised by the leaders, not by the subjects. In addition, such rules are often incorporated in laws, so that they apply to all people, and compliance can be enforced by sanctions. Violation of these rules means that some form of punishment can be imposed, this at the discretion of the leaders or the judicial authorities they have created.

The judges within the Roman Catholic Church administer justice in accordance with canon law, which has been in force for centuries and is still used today, even though it is now used less consistently and more selectively. In a recent example of the latter, the Pope, during his visit to Brazil, threatened to excommunicate politicians if they were to cooperate in legalising abortion; such an action would be unthinkable in Europe and in actual fact, would not have any consequences. The Middle Ages showed us the implications of applying the norms set down in canon law; religious leaders often had huge differences of opinion as to their meaning. A similar course is followed in some other religions. But here religious authorities enter a field that is in fact reserved exclusively to the state by drafting laws that apply equally to all people. In this way religions and their churches become power institutions whose power surpasses that of the state because they gain a grip on people's entire lives. History shows repeated examples of how the two were entangled in lengthy and vehement power struggles. In the most extreme case the result is a theocracy, i.e. the church authorities have won the power struggle with the secular authorities, something we still see happening in some countries today.

In the democratic constitutional state, for the first time in history people took their fate in their own hands and separated church and state for this purpose, so that churches became subordinate to the state and the power of the state would prevail. But this has changed nothing in the relationship of the church with its subjects; after all, the church laws still apply in full and it cannot ruled out that, if democracy does not survive, churches will regain power in the future, thus undoing the separation of church and state. It is important to underscore the fact that religious feelings and religion belong to the playing field of illusion, where there is no such thing as absolute truth, although the churches do claim to have it, and indeed attach to it a wide range of very far-reaching consequences, thus making the power of the churches an eminent example of a caricature of power. This becomes all the more poignant if church leaders can violate, on a large scale and without punishment, general moral standards which they themselves have proclaimed to be church standards, and have often even worked out in detail. Thanks to the power of Western democracies today, Rome is repeatedly forced to pay huge sums of money in a wide variety of currencies all over the world in reimbursement of personal damage (compensation for pain and suffering). This sort of thing has nothing to do with the normal means by which power is exercised, but can only be qualified as pure abuse of power and is therefore punishable by law.

4 Conclusions

For this reason it is good to review once again exactly what we mean by the essential characteristics of human beings as absolute entities in this context.

In the field of communication, it has become clear that churches ought to have more of a sense of perspective, showing that they realise that their core business lies on the playing field of illusion, and that they should steer towards a return to religion in the sense of original religious feelings, as this is the deepest motive for which people turn to religion.

Identity (singularity, character) and individuality are the essential characteristics that pre-eminently stand for loyalty to yourself and respect for others, thus making it possible to live our lives fully in accordance with our own singular identity. From this point of view, it must be regarded as extremely curious that churches think they can forbid people to live their lives in accordance with their sexuality if it deviates from the standard. This is such an extreme intervention in people's very being that it could even be regarded as criminal incitement to self-denial, which has tremendous social consequences. Not allowing a person to be himself or herself is equivalent to erasing one's entire personality, and is this not character assassination or a form of mental abuse (16)? We should see it in the perspective of the unequal treatment of men and women. It is about time to place masculinity and femininity in an entirely different perspective than the usual sexual one. Such practices cannot be justified by saying that the persons concerned have voluntarily joined a church, because the church norms do pretend to be universally valid, and the churches try with their might and main to make this part of daily life. For example, take the power struggle conducted by Rome in the run-up to the Italian referendum on the issue of marriage as an institution for one and all, and the recent clash between Rome and Amnesty International on legalisation of abortion in the event of rape. Think of the prohibition of contraceptives in the context of the fight against AIDS. And what can be called voluntary in such cases (perhaps the majority) when joining the church was not at all voluntary, but merely the result of the fact that your parents made certain choices for you?

The essential characteristic of self-fulfilment (development, the search for meaning) as the ultimate goal in the lives of human beings as absolute entities is in fact what we just discussed when we spoke of religion as the original religious feelings that motivate people in their deepest selves. Our search for meaning is clearly to be taken in the broadest sense of the word, meaning everything that can contribute to self-fulfilment. In this perspective, the significance of the other essential characteristics in relation to self-fulfilment is immediately obvious; on the one hand, it is strictly individually determined, while on the other hand it offers unlimited possibilities.

The essential characteristic of autonomy as self-determination and the related relative freedom means that people, to the exclusion of all others, are in charge of their own lives; they can investigate, make their own choices and take responsibility for them in all matters people must deal with in their lives and for which they must be free to do so. This is entirely contrary to many church views. First of all, there is the church hierarchy and its doctrines, which are taken as the basis for rules and regulations with sanctions for non-obedience, thus making it impossible to make your own choices. The entire system of thought of the churches is one that is intended to be taken over in full and applied by its subjects, resulting in a total loss of autonomy and freedom. This characteristic touches on topics such as pregnancy termination and suicide, situations in which people should basically be free to make the choice best suited to themselves and their circumstances. Naturally, an exception must be made in cases where the interests of third parties play a role. The significance of this characteristic for the other characteristics will be clear. Self-determination and freedom are completely intertwined, calling pre-eminently upon independence, self-investigation, making our own choices and taking our own responsibility, to the exclusion of others.

5 The Eastern philosophies

The Eastern philosophies are much more closely, perhaps completely, aligned with the essential characteristics of human beings as absolute entities. Their basic focus is what people do with their own lives, in which they are shown the way (the path) by which to attain their objectives. Terms such as detachment (letting go) describe the core of how people take themselves as a standard with a certain self-effacing modesty towards others based on a form of self-discipline. This allows them to set boundaries for the first two essential characteristics, so that the others can be fulfilled completely.

Capitalism (consumerism), government and human beings as absolute entities

1 Introduction

All these terms are very closely interrelated. The principle of free enterprise production (capitalism in a broad sense), by now widespread around the world (globalisation), requires a government that sets limits to this freedom. Human beings as absolute entities are part of that system and they can acquire a wide range of products that ensure not only their survival but, certainly in the Western world, a life of luxury. The standard of living in the Western world has since reached unprecedented heights, in contrast to other parts of the world, where people still live in abject poverty. Generally speaking, people do not impose any limitations on themselves in this respect, which only encourages manufacturers to produce more, so that consumers now find themselves in a Walhalla where they can buy without limits (consumerism) (17). This cycle has since infested the rest of the world, which has a great many consequences. All we can do is wait for the time when things will have run their course, but there will be a price to pay, because it seems as good as certain that terrible things will happen, at least if it is not possible to mobilise a powerful enough countermovement that can bring present-day developments to a standstill.

Our recent history has seen repeated attempts to devise solutions for the detrimental consequences of the capitalist system (freedom). Communism (central management, lack of freedom) proved not to be a good alternative; as always, the solution will have to be a happy medium between the extremes of human greed and lack of freedom. The very nature of the capitalist system (without limits) seems to mean that it will not lead to a solution. Nor will the state under the rule of democratic law offer a solution because in fact it can only carry out the will of its citizens, which forms its basis. This means that the only place a solution can be sought is in the citizens themselves (18), but they do not seem sufficiently equipped to deal with it. They have managed to observe that there is a serious problem (19), but are at a loss to find a solution, something outside the box.

The heart of the problem is in fact formed by a type of human behaviour that we refer to as consumerism, the unlimited purchase of all products offered on the markets at all costs and at the expense of all else. These are consumers who have lost their bearings, who are no longer able to impose any restrictions on themselves, not even when they know the serious consequences of their behaviour. In fact they cannot be blamed for such behaviour; after all, they simply allow themselves to be guided by their urge for survival, which means that everything is permitted and that there are no boundaries. And history has shown that people have only allowed restrictions to be imposed on them when they were associated with a religion that imposed certain rules to live by, and obedience could be coerced. But Westerners have lost their faith, so no solution can be expected in that direction. And it is a fact that religions gave their subjects carte blanche when capitalism made its appearance, or at least they ignored the system. As long as their subjects complied with their churchly obligations, they could do as they pleased, and the churches profited greatly from all the benefits that capitalism brought for them as well. In any case this applies to states where a clear separation between church and state has been elevated to the norm, and it immediately explains why poverty is still widespread in theocratic states, and the Western states are now confronted with the consequences.

2 The law of supply and demand

Capitalism is subject to an iron law, the law of supply and demand. Products for which there is no need don't stand a chance on the market. Supply and demand must therefore connect seamlessly, and if not, the price mechanism will ensure that they do. This can even go so far that a product prices itself out of the market because the costs are no longer offset by the benefits. In an endless response to the unlimited needs of people in all respects, products can be put on the market and kept there and consumers can be stimulated to satisfy their relative needs. If we were to make a scale of products corresponding to a certain level of need, running from the primary needs of life to the highly luxurious products (which are not really necessary), it would clearly show how things stand with the fulfilment of people's needs in an absolute sense. The further that boundary is crossed, the more evident it will be that purchase of such a product is no longer justified in relation to the price that must be paid for it in the form of damage to certain interests. In this connection we might ask how far people ought to go, or be allowed to go, in their unrestricted fulfilment of needs and the corresponding production that causes damage to certain interests. In other words, where is the boundary between the necessary fulfilment of the primary needs of life and all other forms of need fulfilment? Human beings as absolute entities have it in their power to set limits and to conduct themselves in accordance with them. To do so, they must make a deliberate choice and act accordingly. But if we are to take responsibility, we must start by investigating this problem and going through the stages so that we can bear the responsibility.

In a general sense, there is no escaping capitalism in this world, but you can limit its detrimental consequences. The ensuing problems are so serious that adequate measures will have to be quite drastic, without damaging the system in the core. They must avoid only the very worst detrimental consequences, the consequences that can threaten our existence, our very survival. There are two ways in which to approach this: individually and collectively.

We can call human beings to account individually, but we can never be certain of achieving the desired result. You can never force people individually, as absolute entities, to exhibit certain behaviour, but you can try to convince them that you are right, so that they will want to change their behaviour; this is a long and difficult road, but it is one that has to be taken. And you can indeed convince people when you can demonstrate that their behaviour forms an obstacle to their primary objective (survival) and their ultimate goal of self-fulfilment through development and the search for meaning. The damage, especially that to the environment in the broadest sense of the word, is a very serious threat to our progeny (19). It is something people can no longer afford to disagree about. Our planet earth and nature, on which we are dependent in our urge for survival, are in danger of being defeated, of losing out, and as we have seen, this would mean the end of human beings as absolute entities because an important link in their origin and evolution, which is also a condition for their existence, is in danger of disappearing. In this field too, people as individuals can band together to make this subject a political item: they can put it on the political agenda with a view to making it a government responsibility through elections, thus calling on the collective to render an accounting and harnessing the power of the state to help solve these problems.

But the very nature of the problems means that only individuals, acting en masse, can make a direct and substantial contribution, and the state can only contribute indirectly, but nonetheless essentially, to possible solutions; individuals can exhibit simple discipline by means of detachment, by letting go of their material state of being, and restricting their urge for survival to a minimum, to only what is strictly necessary (individually determined). This will create considerable scope for any number of developments that can make life worthwhile and lead to ultimate self-fulfilment, so that human beings as absolute entities can make their own contribution to solving this worldencompassing problem. If all people all around the world do this simultaneously by making a deliberate choice, then this altered demand will make it possible to break through the iron law of supply and demand, leading to a snowball effect. In fact this is the only way to bring the problems to a conclusive solution, so at all events we must employ all means and the greatest possible perseverance. Nonetheless, it will be a long-term affair, one involving uncertainty, because we are dealing with a house divided, one to which the use of force is foreign, so that participation must be voluntary. Even so, the flesh is weak. The contribution of the state (the collective) can be supportive in various ways, two of which, from an unexpected angle, will be discussed here.

3 A general prohibition of advertising via the media (radio and television) and Setting radical limits to every form of mobility that causes CO2 emissions

At this point we might well ask how effective the measures proposed by the climate conferences have been. It's quite simple: such measures cannot remove the causes of the problems and can only be seen as ways of alleviating the pain.

First of all it is important to establish that the most immediate cause of the problems is the continually increasing world population: now at eight billion, within the foreseeable future (2050) it will be ten billion (calculation of the United Nations Population Council). Since any measures will have to be voluntary, an effective population policy, such as in China, would not seem to be among the possibilities. In this context, human beings as absolute entities are subjected to forces to which they can offer little or no resistance, namely the urge to reproduce; it is part of our origin and evolution and cannot be regarded as an essential characteristic, as is the urge for survival. Although a population policy will presumably not be able to contribute to a worldwide solution to the problems, it will make mankind aware of their seriousness and so contribute indirectly. No means should be shunned; action must be undertaken on all fronts. However, the growing world population and an adequate population policy are beyond the scope of this book.

A general prohibition of advertising via the media (radio and television)

The object is not to combat capitalism, but to remove its detrimental effects. A general prohibition of advertising in the media will considerably reduce the influence of capitalism. Businesses can manifest themselves via their own channels, for example via the internet, so that they no longer present themselves to consumers, but consumers can seek them out if need be. Advertising (17) in the media has psychological consequences: people are manipulated, are subjected to forms of mental coercion to buy certain products at the expense of other companies that make those same products; as such, it is a weapon in the competition between companies. Advertising has grown into a worldwide billion-dollar industry in which the costs are ultimately paid by consumers (17).

It is not just the advertising that is objectionable, but also the fact that it takes place in the media. In particular, radio and television are means of communication that are outstandingly suited for people to manifest themselves to one another in the broadest sense of the word. Advertising on such media greatly interferes with this. It gives businesses a forum that is not only manipulative, but which has also turned the entire field of broadcasting topsy-turvy: it has taken on a domineering role in this respect (17), not simply determining what people listen to or watch, but becoming a financial determinant as well. As so many things in society are now solely dictated by commercial interests, the interests of viewers and listeners are violated, trampled and subordinated to them. The result is a string of commercial channels that place their own interests (money) first and foremost; channels, furthermore, which show such little difference in the level of their programmes and their advertising that they can be abolished completely. Thanks to the internet, the importance of daily newspapers has declined, and so has the need of involving them in this discussion.

As a result of a general prohibition of advertising in the media, the influence of business (capitalism) on daily life will be drastically reduced, which will not only give people much more peace and quiet, but will also lead to a marked fall in the demand for products, thus affecting supply and leading to considerably less economic activity, which will have favourable consequences for the environment. The demand for luxury articles will collapse, and so the supply of luxury articles will decrease to the same extent. Because of its very nature, the demand for products that satisfy the primary needs of life will remain, with a corresponding level of supply. The companies that make these products can continue to compete as of old, only now without the spurious means of advertising, at least in the media. Companies can certainly present themselves to their potential clients in all other permitted manners. But for consumers, the pressure will be off and consumerism will have been crushed.

Setting radical limits to every form of mobility that causes CO2 emissions

Here lies the actual core of our problem; it is the cause of all forms of pollution (19). Let me simply sidestep the matter of the hole in the ozone layer, worldwide climate change, the rising sea level and the need for higher dikes, because we can continue along those lines for an hour without getting one step further. But what is striking about this is that all over the world people are perfectly willing to fight the last consequences in the chain; they rack their brains and hold conferences and write lengthy reports announcing measures that are referred to as huge challenges for the future, but none of them have the wits or the courage simply to look into the deeper causes, to take those as the starting point and to find solutions that will ask greater discipline and self-restraint of people.

One such solution is setting radical limits to every form of mobility that causes CO2 emissions. Obviously, I realise that you cannot simply abolish these forms of mobility from one day to the next. But you can set limits to their use, and the problems are serious enough to fully justify setting limits that may be perceived as radical. It is of the utmost importance to seek alternatives that do not involve CO2 emissions and until we have such alternatives, this issue must be viewed very pragmatically; but wherever at all possible, we must set limits. To start with, all cars must be barred from the centres of towns, cars for private use and all related products must be made prohibitively expensive, and permits must be required for all business and industrial activities that cause CO2 emissions. The expected increase in the number of cars in the near future (in the Netherlands: from seven million in 2007 to ten million in 2050; calculation of Statistics Netherlands) means it is absolutely necessary to intervene now and not wait any longer. Those cars must not materialise. We must find alternatives. All this is in order to create a better world for our children to live in. Be honest: would you want to live in the world as we can expect it to be if we do not take steps now to alter its present condition, and in which it is foreseeable that disasters are waiting to happen? It is five minutes to twelve, so there is no time for half-hearted measures or procrastination. And then people will discover that they are closer to nature when they walk, cycle and take public transport (which must be expanded and improved) than with one car per family, and equilibrium will have been restored.

The credibility of politics
The absence of an overall vision, manipulation of citizens, bureaucracy and the crisis in party politics

1 Overall vision
Cohesion

For some time, large numbers of people have not made use of their democratic right to vote (20) and have simply lost any interest in politics. Most people have a good life, but politics does not hold much appeal for them. This might perhaps have to do with the lack of cohesion in our everyday life, because religious life as we formerly knew it can no longer offer the same certainty as in the past, and at the same time we now live in a world in which we have everything our heart desires in a material sense, certainly compared to fifty years ago, but in which we have lost ourselves in the process. In such a world, what else can we expect than that our politicians are but unadorned reflections of the emptiness that we experience, because a people gets the politicians it deserves. Members of parliament are meant to reflect and channel subjects that are of interest to people. This is a hard and fast rule; it cannot be otherwise.

What it means is that we must first set to work on ourselves, because politicians show us what we are, and it is hardly anything to write home about. What occupies us right now is the multicultural society and our internal struggle to bring the Islamic faith in conformity with our claimed standards and the values of the democratic constitutional state - but then what? This situation applies to all European countries. All current developments are still related to the consequences of the world wars in the first half of the twentieth century, in which everything was literally and figuratively broken down, razed to the ground, demolished. Nothing was left of what had been; everything had to be rebuilt, and it was, but we lost our faith in ourselves in the process. Rooted as we were in the Judeo-Christian tradition, it is questionable whether we can be proud of this. Those who are still part of that tradition are surprised by the lack of understanding and count their blessings.

But what does this leave for the masses of people who have the feeling that they are empty-handed? They too are entitled to a meaningful existence, and this takes on substance entirely outside of the democratic state under the rule of law. What religions actually do: on the one hand, they pay lip service to the separation of church and state, but on the other hand they do their utmost to translate their religious ideas into political terms and carry them out. If this is implemented to the extreme, it leads to a state with theocratic leanings, one that controls all of life - but I seem to recall that in a democracy we have sworn off that sort of thing.

And so we should, because such states are based on their so-called Holy Books; viewed alone or together, they are capable of multiple interpretations. You definitely need to ask yourself how much of them is true and whether they can give sufficiently clear answers to contemporary issues facing large sections of humanity. Unfortunately, to find a solution to this dilemma, it is no longer possible to trust blindly on the truths said to have been revealed by God; we must undertake a critical investigation of ourselves and take responsibility for our findings, no longer squirming to sidestep them (33).

We can reasonably assume that the distinctions we have made (origin and evolution, essential characteristics and experience), as they are related and have been elaborated, are certain (33) (44) and can serve as a basis for all people all over the world, which includes religions. The only difference with religions is their assumption of an extra dimension which they see as having certain consequences, but this does not alter the basis, so we can disregard that aspect here. In fact it is thanks to this that their equality is possible; they can exist alongside one another in an authentic manner (Dialogues 1). The distinctions made provide us with the cohesion that we are so in need of at present, and we stand to gain by assuming that they are credible because they are rooted in our deepest essence and our conviction in this respect.

2 Actions speak louder than words
Direct contact between voters and their representatives

In addition, politics can garner greater credibility by actually carrying out social proposals that have been translated into political terms and incorporated in the programmes of political parties, by making them part of the government's responsibility (actions speak louder than words). If a general prohibition of advertising via the media can make a fundamental contribution to combating consumerism, then it should also apply to politics, and political parties and politicians should no longer profile themselves towards citizens (voters) only via the media, but should also speak to them directly, in direct contact; they need to directly explain their political ideas, which will allow citizens to assess the authenticity of their political statements and to test their credibility in a more general sense.

The most important objection to conducting politics via the media is the psychological manipulation of voters (a form of exercising power) in this way. Communication in the media is only about 'image-building'; the reality on which this is based (hot air) does not play a role. Voters are unerringly aware of this; they feel betrayed, and the credibility of politics is at issue. If there is also too much discrepancy between bureaucracy and everyday life, then people's trust in politics quickly sinks very low, and this is the situation at present.

The essence of democracy is the direct contact between voters and those they elect. Democracy is an achievement that we spent centuries of physical and mental struggle fighting for. Nowadays, when the media serve as the main point of contact with voters, this so hard-fought achievement is simply thrown away, and the very roots of democracy are corroded, which has far-reaching consequences.

The proof of this statement is found in the example given in the country where democracy was first established in both a factual and a legal sense, the United States of America, where the presidential elections always start in the state of Iowa in the face-to-face contact of all presidential candidates with their voters to gain their favour. Not only do they show themselves in public, but they visit voters at home and converse with them in the street about everyday life, the problems they face day by day - direct contact, from person to person, where they can look one another straight in the eye, shake hands and feel each other's physical and human warmth, which ultimately makes it possible for both to assess who is the right man or woman to bring changes into the voters' lives, so that the problems that really matter to them can be resolved. For years, the example set here for the other states has meant that the candidate who wins the elections in Iowa stands the biggest chance to become President of the United States.

3 Government organisation

In connection with the credibility of politics, the role of the government organisation itself surely may not go unmentioned. Although formally speaking, the Dutch cabinet and parliament are part of it, it nevertheless plays an independent role of great importance. I mentioned the discrepancy between bureaucracy and the everyday life of ordinary people, which has reduced the credibility of politics to a minimum for them.

This gap is caused by a number of factors, such as:

1. Bureaucracy is continually expanding (autonomously), even without a corresponding increase in its duties and responsibilities (this seems to be a law of economics), while the quality of the work it produces does not visibly improve - it sooner declines, so that from this perspective one might say that the government organisation has become top-heavy. In other words, there is an imbalance between the size of the government organisation and its duties and the quality of the work it delivers, which puts increasing pressure on the private sector, including business, in the form of stifling regulations that constantly grow in magnitude.

2. The absence of sufficient means by which to control and monitor the performance of duties and responsibilities, both within the government organisation and outside of it, so that government seems to produce an endless stream of failures, often only brought to light retrospectively and painfully by parliamentary inquiries or committees of elder statesmen (20) when the irreparable damage has already been done; fresh in our memories are contracting and road construction and more recently, bridge building and education, to name just a few; but also a poorly functioning Tax Administration which tries to disguise this in publicity that seems to suggest the contrary; and then there is the credit crisis.

3. Developments in society on which the government has insufficient grasp or even none at all, and thus always seems to be at a loss as to how to deal with them effectively, e.g. the growing number of motor cars: forecast for many years, the anticipated figures have since been reached, to which the government response has simply been to build more roads (and nowhere near enough), and costly experiments to pay for road use that seem to benefit only the treasury, while it apparently does not occur to anyone

to do something about the cars instead; another example would be developments in relation to globalisation.

4. The conflict of interests on the part of government when it must take action against interests in which it is itself involved or is even dependent on, such as putting a stop to or at least regulating all activities that result in CO_2 emissions, but neglects to take such measures because then it would lose hundreds of billions of euros in income, so that its policy can only be qualified as two-faced.

4 The two-party system

The political parties have been in a state of crisis for years, and not without reason. The confessional parties first saw it coming and very early on decided to join forces and go forward as one party. But the Conservatives and the Socialists are still at an impasse, which is disappointing for voters, because the Christian Democrats use this to their benefit in power ploys, continually playing the two out against each other. It can be regarded as a relic from bygone political eras. After all, for many years Christians have been members of all political parties, and religion is no longer decisive in choosing a party, although the Christian Democrats would all too gladly support it with a view to political gain. Nor can Christian Democrats be viewed as a middle-of-the-road party, but they are accorded this qualification thanks to the presence of the other two sides.

What is worse, the views of all three parties can be deemed to be obsolete. The Christian Democrats in fact have a conservative basis and certain socially minded leanings, which they ascribe to their Christian ideals but which could equally well be derived from more universal human motives. Both the Conservatives and the Socialists also have a conservative basis and differ solely in their approach to the social elements, which might be termed conservative and progressive respectively. There is no longer much difference in the content; the only difference is the speed at which societal developments are to be managed, so there are no further obstacles to developing a two-party system. From this point of view, the Christian Democrats have always felt more at home in the conservative camp and they get along significantly less well with the socialists, so the choice will be an easy one.

The crisis in party politics is palpable every day, recently becoming particularly topical. On both the left and the right, the traditional political parties are being overrun by parties that emerge from social movements that want to see policy become more conservative or more progressive.

To end this impasse, a broad progressive front must be created that will drive the conservatives together and break open the present political system, so that it is possible to make a fundamental choice, and the party or the side that wins the elections will be able to take the responsibilities of government upon itself and not spend many months playing power games leading to a less than satisfactory (and less than transparent) result; nowadays you never know for sure whether your vote is actually put to the use for which you cast it. This will put credibility back in politics. And there need be no objection to this. It will not result in throwing away ideas that are allegedly Christian Democratic, Conservative or Socialist. In the course of our political history, such principles were long ago imbued in the government organisation which currently determines our lives, and they have been set down in legislation and legal principles whose application and development will be very carefully supervised by the judicial authorities: one might even say that our democracy has entered the next phase on its way to political maturity.

VI Afterword

In this afterword I must ask myself how it differs from the foreword, or in other words, what is the added value of what I have tried to express on the pages between them?

In this context I would like to stress the fact that I am neither a professional philosopher nor a philosophical anthropologist, and my approach to philosophy and philosophical anthropology is solely determined by an enormous personal interest in these sciences. I must therefore observe that my work cannot be qualified as a form of academic discourse, and so I have avoided any academic discussion and only put forth my own personal ideas about my concept of human beings as absolute entities because it is my belief that elaborating this touches on a fundamental human truth, one that I have not found in most philosophies, which I regard as a serious shortcoming and which I feel should be provided in.

When human beings search for themselves and for truth, the problem is that, from their own empirical involvement, they first look around themselves in their everyday world, where they encounter themselves and others, but then they start shifting the boundaries towards a presumed invisible, abstract, interior and external world. This automatically leads to a great many questions, questions to which all people try to find their own answers. In that invisible world you might, for example, conclude that there is a God and/or an inner self (soul, mind, etc.), but clearly, a problem arises as soon as you bring in the visible, concrete world, because who or what is God and the inner self; how should we picture them? Where do they live, where are they situated in the whole of things, where can we find them and perhaps, how are they related? But we have no answers to these questions, because they are part of the world of the imagination, a world in which everything is possible, but impossible at the same time. So there is nothing to be gained by looking around there and if you do, you will always find insoluble problems and huge confusion.

My starting point is therefore human beings in their empirical involvement with their own origin and evolution, from which they have emerged (as absolute entities). The problems just cited led me to believe that we have no clear and unambiguous definition of the concept of experience, which prompted me to devote much attention to this. The definition of this concept is thus a substantial part of my treatise. From our history and experience we can deduce our origin and evolution in broad lines, as well as the defining essential characteristics of human beings as absolute entities. From this starting point, I have developed my theme in respect of a number of everyday topics.

In my philosophy of man I restrict myself to systematising and describing the innermost essence of human beings with the object of entering into a dialogue in that respect (22)(33)(Dialogues 1)(38) so as to attain a better understanding of matters that could serve as a basis for the most divergent philosophical and mundane topics, without which we would find ourselves in a vacuum, thus merely serving to increase the present confusion. I am aware of the fact that my assumptions may not all have been proven scientifically, which means that we are still fumbling in the dark, so to speak, in many respects. We will therefore have to be patient (21), but I am convinced that the direction I have chosen is the right one (22)(33)(Dialogues 1)(38)(47).

VII Summary in English and Chinese

Summary

To summarise, human beings as absolute entities have undergone developments over millions of years (they have evolved) so that today we can point to a number of traits (essential characteristics) in connection with their nature and origin, which we have looked at from a point of view that we generally call empirical reality (the process of experience). In this process our empirical involvement can be regarded as the motor that has made us, or caused us to develop, into what we are today. This is our everyday reality. This alone has given us our essential characteristics (urge for survival, communication, identity, self-fulfilment, self-determination), and these essential characteristics can be seen as the motives - which have proved in the course of history to be enduring - for our actions. This implies that they do not truly exist, but they apparently typify our most original state of being, set down in billions of cells (matter) that make us who we are.

It follows from the nature of human beings as absolute entities that the way in which they get along with each other is primarily determined by the free interplay of forces. They can impose limitations (self-limitations, voluntarily) on themselves for the sake of peace (conscience) and can avail themselves of norms (rules of morals and decency) as guidelines for their actions. This involves the relationships between individuals in contrast to individuals in a group (family and friends, clubs, companies, religious communities, government) where the group imposes norms (rules of morals and decency, mores, customs and usages, laws) on its participants, who must adhere to them.

We can thus conclude that the free interplay of forces (absolute freedom) is inherent in human nature, that any limitation of this is alien to human nature and that the use of norms is only prompted by a need for ordering, depending on the circumstances (efficiency), when there is a clash of interests. This absolute freedom in connection with the realisation of the total of all essential characteristics of human beings as absolute entities in relation to others must be distinguished from the relative freedom of people in realising their autonomy in the form of self-determination, which is limited in this sense.

小结

扼要言之，经过数百万年的发展过程(发展史)之后，如今的“人”已经成为了一个个绝对的独立存在体，从而使我们能够根据“从经验观察中所获得的感知(经验过程)”而指出我们“人”在天性和本源方面的若干特征。我们“人”所进行的经验参与可以被视为使我们能够发展到如今状态的引擎；这些所谓经验参与便是我们日复一日对现实的感知。我们的各种天性纯粹是可以从我们的本源而察知的，这些天性也显然在历史上形成了我们各种行为的动机，因此它们并非是一种现实存在，而是属于我们最原始的组元部分，即存留于好几十亿个使我们之所以是我们“人”的细胞之内。

鉴于人具有“绝对独立存在体”的属性，他们自然就主要是以作为“力量自由发挥”的结果而相互关联在一起的。他们可以为了和平(天良)而在这种相互关联内施加一定的限制(自主性自我限制)，并可以采用各种规范和标准(那些我们称之为道德和得体行为的规则)作为行为准则。这就使我们遇到了“个人之间的关系”对立于向成员施行集体规范(道德和情理、风俗和习惯及法律)的“集体内关系”(家人和朋友、协会和会所、事业、教堂及政府)的问题。

由此我们可以导出：力量的自由发挥 (绝对自由)与人类的天性有着内在的关联，对其进行任何限制都是与其不相容的，而施用规范和标准纯粹是因为在出现利益冲突时为了获得一定意义上的秩序而针对具体情形(目标)的一种所为。这一涉及“实现人作为相对于他人的绝对独立存在体之所有需求”的自由，应该与以实现自主(自决)为目标的人的(相对)自由进行区别，后者自有其特定的界限范围。

VIII Humanism (36) **and philosophy**

A new philosophy of man as the basis for a humanist ideology, with its roots in America: its origins and where it now stands (James Joseph Dagenais 1923-1981)

"The only claims which philosophy can make to leadership in the total enterprise of understanding man is its capacity to explicitate its own presuppositions ... if the necessary presuppositions of a philosophy of man can be clarified and justified, its claim to be basic can be validated..... The presuppositions of any philosophy, I maintain, involve a fundamental attitude towards myself, the other, and the world. The most fundamental evidence here is that *the universe is not a thing, nor even a system of things, not an object or a system of objects, but primordially an interpersonal world, a world of and for persons.*

Philosophy can then be defined as a reflection upon the pre-reflexive, pre-philosophical, pre-scientific *experiencing* of being, that is, upon experiencing before any kind of conscious thematization. If philosophy is a radical and transcendental thinking, that is, a thinking upon the *a priori* conditions of possibility of all thinking and all experiencing, then the experiencing which is reflected upon must be experiencing in the largest sense. It is the experiencing in my insertion of being – concretely, the experiencing of myself and the other in the world."

(James Joseph Dagenais 1923-1981) (37)

1 Philosophical Anthropology: a consistent overall vision of man and his world

This definition can largely be derived from a study of the basic tenets of the relationship between philosophy and the sciences, in particular the philosophy of man and the social sciences in *Models of Man, A Phenomenological Critique of Some Paradigms in the Human Sciences* by Jim Dagenais (38), from which, in a nutshell, the following hypotheses are borrowed:

"The thesis maintained is that the human sciences, as sciences, must attempt to reduce the meaning of man to the control of the scientific presuppositions which found each science, and that, in consequence, each scientific model can and must pretend to universal exclusiveness. Furthermore, since each science must be limited to one perspective, they cannot all be summed up under the control of another science, such as philosophy. This amounts to saying that the sciences (positive, axiomatic, or humanistic) must be autonomous as sciences; that the only critique of them as sciences is from within the sciences themselves. Any other knowledge we have of human beings outside of these sciences is, in respect to them, unscientific."

Dagenais then gives three possible answers to the question "… how we know human being…", of which he explicitly chooses the second one:

"First, … through the sciences of man….. But, again, each of these sciences is autonomous and independent … Second, we might hypothesize that we know man through a "definition" of man. But then the elaboration of an all-encompassing theory about human being would have to depend upon all the empirical sciences anyway. Otherwise it would have only the apodicticity of a logically necessary statement. That is, if it is to be about real human beings, such a theory will have to depend upon a host of extra-systematic assumptions which will serve only to invalidate the supposed logical consistency of the argument. Third, … through a prestructured "metaphysical system" of the whole….. This really makes the sciences of man unnecessary and gratuitous, and explains nothing about the origin of the system in any case."

Ultimately he comes to the conclusion that "[i]n all these inadequate hypotheses there is one recognizable constant: that all understanding of human being in the world, whether scientific or philosophical, is founded upon a pre-scientific and pre-philosophical experiencing of human beings as self-and-other-in-the-world. The only alternative, then, is a critical explicitation of this experiencing; and that is the task of philosophy. It is the task undertaken in this essay, especially in the important and basic defense of the second phase of the thesis stated above."

He describes "the present status of philosophical anthropology" as follows:
"It is difficult to write on a subject which hardly exists, except in the spirits of its practitioners."(3) "In the English-speaking world there are no Chairs of Philosophical Anthropology, and courses with the title are rare. The philosopher, it seems, has some reason to expect the accusation poaching in the fields of the "true" anthropologist, or economist, or what-have-you, since he shares the data of their sciences with them."(2)

"The notion of a philosophical anthropology did not spring into existence suddenly, without antecedents. The subject is an outgrowth of what used to be called, in some circles, 'philosophical psychology', and more recently, 'the philosophy of man'. Philosophical psychology was an outgrowth of the Scholastic enterprise of 'rational psychology', a manual treatment of the peculiarly epistemological and psychological works of Thomas Aquinas (for example, the treatise of *de Veritate*, or the commentaries upon Aristotles' *de Anima*). In the course of time, the manuals were retouched, reorganised or remodelled, keeping the basic Aristotelian and Thomistic orientation, together, often, with the Kantian-Thomistic synthesis of Maréchal. Lonergan, Coreth, Rahner, Lotz and Donceel, among others, have been the guiding lights of this movement in modern times; but the movement, with all its accretions, its growing respect for 'existentialism' and 'phenomenology', its increasing abandonment of antiquated terminology, still searches for 'what makes man properly man', perhaps for an 'essence'.

But in the context of the '*philosophia perennis*', in which essence is constituted through genus and specific difference, the old definition of man as 'rational animal' no longer suffices, and the effort at explicitating the definition with the help of modern scientific experimentation succeeds only in demonstrating the inadequacy of the original definition. For example, Joseph Donceel's completeness and universality; any knowledge that we might have of 'man' outside of the knowledge that we have of him in any of these sciences is simply 'unscientific' from the point of view of the science involved. The option of the present book is that the final explanation of 'man' lies **outside** [emphasis added by author] of *all* the possible scientific views of him because it lies within the *origins* of any and all the sciences, including the science of philosophy." (33)

"The currently fashionable models of man appear to some to be reductivist (the 'no-thing but' type of explanation); but, in fact, we cannot expect them to be anything else. Such models, through their own coherence and rigor of the methods which in their elaboration, make a claim to ultimacy, and we had to take them seriously. It is difficult to impress the importance of this view upon beginners in philosophy; we owe to Edmund Husserl, in his operation of the 'transcendental reduction', and his 'bracketing of the world of the *natural attitude*', the sole possibility we have of bringing to consciousness the realization that we possess a non-scientific pre-knowledge of our world and of ourselves which we are explicitating through our objective scientific endeavors. Without the transcendental focus, such consciousness would simply 'go without saying', and we would never have explicit knowledge that there is the possibility of reflection", (33) "and consequently, the 'objective view' of the universe which we have scientifically would be the only one possible.

There is, then, a series of questions which must be answered here, or at least a series of problems which must be clearly distinguished. The first question is one of perspective. It was said above that 'many sciences study man'. Traditionally speaking, each of these sciences chooses a perspective which constitutes the 'formal object' of the science in question. There is thus one clue provided for the success of the enterprise of philosophical anthropology: there is only one object, properly speaking, the 'material object', man himself. But the initial problem also arises here; a material object cannot be studied 'in itself', but only under the modality of some formal perspective.
Consequently, to carry out the implications of the task, it seems that one must add that this one object should be treated from all possible points of view. True enough, and that will make the enterprise a truly interdisciplinary one." (33) "However, one must be careful not to reintroduce incoherence through eclecticism, that is, by adopting simultaneously incompatible or contradictory points of view. This, in my opinion, is the heart of the problem, and the precise fault of the 'human sciences', taken as an agglomerate, today.

... it may be true that an 'object' (of study) is the sum total, or total structure, of all possible perspectives upon it ...

Is it, then, possible, as an alternative problematic, to lay the groundwork for a philosophy of man which can, in turn, serve as a groundwork for the sciences of man by uncovering the vectors determining the horizon within which the data are accessible? Such a project is indeed possible, since, in any case, philosophical presuppositions (unexplicated evidence) lie at the origin of all sciences. But the assertion of this possibility carries a *proviso*: Provided philosophy itself be included in the class of sciences obliged to clarify their own presuppositions and to justify them. If philosophers can be clear about their own presuppositions, and justify them, they shall have a coherent basis upon which to launch a critical study of the various claims to define man ... the basic presuppositions of such a philosophy of man ... may... serve as a unifying 'point of view' which informs all the perspectives upon man without compromising the methodologies and formal aspects proper to each one.

... presuppositions ... unreflected or forgotten evidences ... philosophy is best equipped to achieve some clarity about its own presuppositions..... perhaps 'option' is the best word to use when choosing a perspective for philosophy, and 'attitude' is the best term for its method. The option ... is that a philosophy of man, a 'philosophical anthropology', is the only [one] relevant today.

The only claims which philosophy can make to leadership in the total enterprise of understanding man is its capacity to explicitate its own presuppositions ... the foundation of science is always *relative to the science* in question, and not to any ultimate or absolute foundation; the latter is found only through an investigation of the ultimate sources of all knowledge. Thus, if the necessary presuppositions of a philosophy of man can be clarified and justified, its claim to be basic can be validated..... The presuppositions of any philosophy, I maintain, involve a fundamental attitude towards myself, the other, and the world. The most fundamental evidence here is that *the universe is not a thing, nor even a system of things, not an object or a system of objects, but primordially an interpersonal world, a world of and for persons*. The problem of these persons is that they have constituted a world of objects and then have forgotten the act of constitution. In our world of technological objectivity, the human person, as the originator of objectivity, has become confused with his own creation. Our inability to remember our act of creation is coterminous with our inability to remember having forgotten. The main point ... then, is an effort to remember, perhaps by negation more than by affirmation, what are the ineffaceable bench marks of our passage through the world in which persons are in communication.

Regarding 'myself': ... the Ego as originator of the totality of the significance of the personal and natural world. Now, however, it is clear that 'I' (the 'I' of the 'Cogito') cannot be the starting point in philosophical investigation. Both the presuppositionless beginning and the absolute beginning implied in 'my' being the starting-point of philosophy are impossible. The absolute beginning involves the question, 'Can I know anything?'..... The response ... consists in returning to what is thought to be the least contestable minimum of affirmation as a starting-point in philosophy, and implies one or other variation of the *cogito* argument. (St. Augustine used it even before Descartes.)

Heidegger, in our time, has traced the history of the failure of the absolute beginning of a philosophy which asserts that the primordial evidence in human knowledge is 'I think' and the illusory conclusion, 'therefore I am'. 'I am' is precisely not an epistemological statement nor a logical conclusion, for it is the very presupposition of one's thinking. The primordial reference to 'I am' as an ontological statement rather than to 'I think' as an epistemological statement is, then, a first step. A second step is to ask where precisely, I am. Heidegger's apparently simple answer is that I am simply 'there'; and this is the beginning of his ontological analysis of how it is that I am there, and what is the mode of my being there..... The impossibility of an absolute beginning entails the impossibility of a presuppositionless beginning, since we can at least recognize the primordial reference to being in all knowledge and affirmation.....

Philosophy can then be defined as a reflection upon the pre-reflexive, pre-philosophical, pre-scientific experiencing of being, that is, upon experiencing before any kind of conscious thematization. If philosophy is a radical and transcendental thinking, that is, a thinking upon the a priori conditions of possibility of all thinking and all experiencing, then the experiencing which is reflected upon must be experiencing in the largest sense. It is the experiencing in my insertion of being concretely, the experiencing of myself and the other in the world.

Now that the discussion has returned to the level of metaphysical presuppositions (options), we might reflect upon the 'we are' in relation to 'the world'. This is the third panel in the tryptich of necessary presuppositions in the philosophy of man.

Here, some care will be necessary in order to be clear; for epistemologically the reader may be tempted to fall back into a sterile nineteenth-century idealist position and 'construct' the world, and psychologically and ethically to espouse a current and popular 'existentialism' in which the creation of the universe can be an arbitrary matter. There is something to be said for both these points of view, however, provided that something is said with discretion. The present proposal is to define human consciousness, with Husserl, not as a thing but as a giver of meaning, and to define man in a preliminary way not as a 'rational animal' but as essentially project and as incarnate freedom." (cf. Chapter XIII Core Concepts, Essential (Relative Freedom))

"The intention in doing so is to surpass both idealism and existentialism by subjecting both consciousness and project to a reality principle, and to make an incorporation of the non-voluntary and the non-sense (or contradiction and alienation) in the human situation an essential part of the incarnation of human liberty. The questions, 'Are we *completely* free?' and 'Are we *utterly* determined?' are both nonsense. The meaning given to the world is thus man's meaning, and the creation of the world by man is the creation of a human universe, in the sense of both a community of human persons and a human landscape." (cf. Michael Frayn, note (5)). "The 'we are', then, who are in the world to begin with, find our meaning already in the world; and we define our project as part of an emergent humanity.

With this perspective, I think, the *de facto* intention of both project and emergence can be determined (I do not say it is an easy task!), and deviations from the hopes incarnated in the project, whether due to fault or fallibility, can be uncovered." (cf. Chapter XIII, Core Concepts)

"There are theological and ethical corollaries to this thesis, which may be set aside for future elaboration; the main corollary in this context is epistemological, indicating that knowledge, as well as behavior, is primarily social in character. The empiricist *tabula rasa* is both unfruitful and misleading, belonging to a context in which absolute beginnings were thought possible." (cf. Chapter XIII, Core Concepts, Relational (Absolute Freedom))

2 Humanism: a philosophy of man championed by Jaap van Praag (1911 - 1981) and Reinout Bakker (1920 - 1987), both following in the footsteps of Dagenais

Jaap van Praag

What Jim Dagenais put forward in his Models of Man had been expressed in broad lines in Jaap van Praag's earlier inaugural speech on humanism as endowed professor of humanism and anthropology of humanism at Leiden University on behalf of the Socrates Foundation of the Dutch Humanist League in 1965 (39) (40):

"We might perhaps best characterise humanism by pointing to the attitude of mind that precedes all theory and practice. The term attitude of mind comprises an element of mental orientation, of awareness of duty. This is where all that which is shared in humanism resides: being seized of a fundamental truth of life; adopting this starting point that goes before every philosophy, or world view, or attitude to life. A person may hold a certain view, but an attitude of mind characterises a person's being. Together with the representation of human beings and the world, which have their origins in this starting point, it constitutes man's philosophy of life. A philosophy of life, then, is a complex of representations for which a particular attitude of mind is the starting point for a world view and a view of man." (44)

"Humanistics involves reasoning through the humanist philosophy of life itself. It contemplates a philosophical pursuit. However, it must do justice to the many and varied philosophical interpretations of humanism, which in itself is also remarkably multiform. And so it will come down to uncovering, wherever possible, the elements that make up the core of all humanism..... In other words: it is a search for the underlying tenets of humanism. And humanistics involves reasoning through the humanist philosophy of life from a phenomenological point of view." (41)

In his farewell lecture in 1979 (42) he put this in more concrete terms in the following formulation, which is based in part on the text of Dagenais, primarily concerning "the final explanation of 'man'":

"In an instructive book, a certain Dagenais attempted to investigate how the scientific models of man related to psychology and sociology; he started with Wundt and Durkheim as representatives of the 'objective' and Brentano and Weber as representatives of the 'subjective' school of thought. 'The option of the present book', he wrote, 'is that the final explanation of "man" lies **outside** [emphasis added by author] of all the possible scientific views of him because it lies within the origins of any and all the sciences, including the science of philosophy.' (33) 'If it now appears that the philosophy of man, even cleansed of its dogmas, cannot work without presuppositions, then after all philosophy is best equipped to achieve some clarity as to his own presuppositions. In this final analysis, perhaps "option" is the best word to use when choosing a perspective for philosophy, and "attitude" is the best term for its method'. And with these quotations we are back at our starting point: the foundations of thinking about man and his world", which are "... the mental attitudes and the postulated models of them" (cf. Chapter XIII, Core Concepts) ... "that can serve as orientation patterns", of which "the constructive capacity can become apparent: their capacity to appreciate and to criticise starting positions, for example in the sciences" (cf. Chapter I, Dialogues 1-7). "This seems to me to be a task of philosophical anthropology as well. Philosophical anthropology can thus be of service to the entire range of knowledge of a university."

Reinout Bakker

In his reflections on philosophical anthropology, Reinout Bakker nowhere refers directly to Jim Dagenais. However, he does refer twice to Jaap van Praag: in his *Wijsgerige antropologie van de twintigste eeuw* (3)(33) and in his farewell speech (33), in which he included verbatim part of a quote from Dagenais cited by Van Praag, particularly in relation to "the final explanation of 'man'":

In the Introduction to the first part he gives the following explication:

"I just used the term 'view of man'. It is impossible to avoid giving a provisional and broad description of what, in my view, is the essence of anthropology, a sort of working hypothesis, which must be tested over and over again using the research questions of this century. It reads: Philosophical anthropology is a part of philosophical thought that deals with the question of man, man as a unity of body, soul and mind, man in relation to himself, the other, society, the world and God. It cannot be practised without the help of human sciences such as psychology, educational theory and sociology; in short, it can only be discussed in an interdisciplinary sense. It should be pointed out that philosophical anthropology must be distinguished from other forms of anthropology, such as biological and cultural anthropology. They will be discussed now and then in this study because they show a good deal of overlap with philosophical anthropology. But what defines the character of philosophical anthropology in comparison to the other forms is the specific fact that it takes its theme and seeks that which constitutes our typical human being-ness in statements that are presumed to be true and accepted as taken for granted in man's knowledge by biological and cultural anthropology as well as by many sciences."(44) "Because of this, philosophical anthropology is a domain unto itself, and cannot be replaced by any other anthropology. In other words: the final explanation of man lies outside all possible scientific views of man that have ever been formulated, because it lies within the origins of every branch of science, including the science of philosophy. 'Philosophical anthropology is neutral', according to Van Praag, 'in that it does not aim to defend a dogma and even less to serve as propaganda for a conviction, but it can scrutinise its own convictions and starting points as well as those of other disciplines, although here a person's own conviction inevitably remains his starting point.'" (43) "It is for this reason that I tend to regard philosophical anthropology as a sort of transcendental philosophy because it is the final ground on which the philosophies, of any nature whatsoever, can be practised implicitly or explicitly."

In his farewell speech (33) he summarised the entire complex of factors that constitute philosophical anthropology:

"... philosophical anthropology is a domain unto itself, and cannot be replaced by any other anthropology. The final explanation of man lies **outside** all possible scientific views that have ever been formulated, because they lie within the origins of every branch of science, including the science of philosophy. It is the final ground on which the philosophies, of any nature whatsoever, can be practised implicitly or explicitly (see R. Bakker. *Wijsgerige antropologie van de twintigste eeuw*. Assen, 2 1982, 3; cf. J. van Praag Levensovertuiging, filosofie en wetenschap, 1979).

In my inaugural speech of 25 January 1965 I spoke of the necessary collaboration between philosophy and science. Philosophy without contact with the empirical sciences is empty, but also: the empirical sciences are blind without the contribution of philosophy. If one of these two poles is made absolute, the danger of gross one-sidedness, or even distortion, is imminent. The fact that the ultimate questions about man are so rarely asked stems from the practice of giving the scientific foundation of philosophy an absolute status. Many phenomenologists and existentialists have warned against such scientism ...

The methods of a post-modern philosophical anthropology will have to be based on reflection, on the claim that it is possible to debate differences and contrasts on reasoned grounds, and on the individual responsibility for the decisions we all make for ourselves in respect of changes in body and mind. A post-modern version of Sartre's creed: man is and always will be what he makes of himself."

3 Dagenais and Chan-fai Cheung (46)

"Max Scheler, in his *Man's Place in Nature*, maintains that there are three most fundamental ideas of man in Western history: man is understood as a rational animal in the Greek philosophy of Plato and Aristotle; as a creature created by God in His image from the Jewish-Christian tradition, and finally as the recent product of animal evolution. In traditional Chinese culture, the dominant ideas of man may be limited to two: the Confucian moral man and the Daoist natural man. Taking the two traditions as a whole, we have therefore two more basic ideas of man to be added to Scheler's list: in addition to the philosophical, the theological and the scientific, there are the moral and finally the natural (Daoist) man. These ideas cannot be all true since they are in fact incompatible with one another in their fundamental philosophical tenets. There is simply no unified idea of man. Here is where Heidegger's critique comes in. Although his "phenomenological destruction" of the metaphysics is only directed to the Western tradition, his critique of the metaphysical basis of the very conception of human nature is, in my opinion, trans-cultural", in the words of Dr. Cheung Chan Fai, professor of philosophy at the Chinese University of Hong Kong in his *Human Nature and Human Existence - On the Problem of the Distinction Between Man and Animal*. (47)

After he establishes what Heidegger "has written in Chapter 9 of Being and Time: 'The "essence" (*Wesen*) of Dasein lies in its existence (*Existenz*)'", his final opinion is that "the major issue is to understand what human being is. Any metaphysical distinction of man drawn from a comparison between man and animals does not really think of man as man in his Being. 'Metaphysics thinks of man on the basis of *animalitas* and does not think in the direction of his *humanitas*'", citing Heidegger's *Letter on Humanism*; "[t]*he essentia* (*Wesen*) of man does not point to the substantia, the whatness, in man. '*Wesen*' means the disclosing process of the understanding of Being (*Seinsverständnis*) in the human Dasein. 'Wesen' - essence - in this sense refers not to the what but the how of Dasein with respect to its 'existence'. The comparison of Aristotle with Xunzi and with Mencius is to show the similar approaches to the question of man, though the two great Confucians place the primacy of the human nature on the moral awareness and its actualization. These two ideas from Aristotle and the Confucians have been the most important for all subsequent theories of man. Heidegger's philosophy has changed all these. The distinction of man from animals should not be sought in human nature but in the meaning of human existence in the light of Being."

The distinction between man and animals as the basis for his study and his invocation of the biological anthropologist Max Scheler immediately earns him some measured criticism from Reinout Bakker (3)(33): "Scheler did not see that philosophical anthropology is an integrational philosophical discipline, in which metaphysics must be consistently excommunicated from the mind. Because it is not useful in a scientific sense ... the study of man in comparison with animals, prominent in the first half of this century, no longer yields up any meaningful results. The 'added value' of man is not expressed in this comparative study. The required empirical method cannot respond to this factor, because it cannot be tested empirically..... And how can one in fact start from a comparison between man and animals if the particular character of the actual comparison is not assessed at the same time? If one wishes to demonstrate that man is fundamentally superior to animals, then one must assume that this can only be proved by means of reflections of man on himself, reflections on the basis of which man is aware of himself as an 'I' that can study both himself and animals."

In respect of Dagenais's *Models of Man* (38) Cheung remarks: "There are indeed many more different theories of man not only within philosophy but also in modern social sciences. Sociology, psychology and anthropology all propose different empirical theories of man, in contrast to the *speculative* ideas in philosophy. The modern discipline of philosophical anthropology is devoted to the synthesis of speculative and empirical theories", only to conclude that "[t]he arguments between all these theories of human nature seem to rest on the justification of the primordiality of the human essence in question." Even after a comprehensive discussion of Max Scheler's *Spirit and Person*, he again reaches the conclusion that "[t]here is still no unified theory of man". This naturally also applies to the solution which he has chosen, namely "... the meaning of human existence in the light of Being" as the basis for "the distinction of man from animals".

But if we sever the link between these two, then what we retain is "... the meaning of human existence in the light of Being", which is precisely what Dagenais says at the end of his essay, where he cites Husserl: "The present proposal is to define human consciousness, with Husserl, not as a thing but as a giver of meaning, and to define man in a preliminary way not as a 'rational animal' but as essentially project and as incarnate freedom." (cf. Chapter XIII, Core Concepts, Essential (Relative Freedom))
They thus take different paths to arrive at the same conclusion, the difference being that Dagenais adds an essential element, incarnate freedom, of which he gives a comprehensive explanation, which is the answer to the question of "what makes man properly man", as described in his *Models of Man*.

In this work, Dagenais laid the theoretical foundation for a new philosophy of man, or philosophical anthropology, but he also explicitly said that it needed to be elaborated in a practical (i.e. concrete) sense: "With this perspective, I think, the *de facto* intention of both project and emergence can be determined (I do not say it is an easy task!), and deviations from the hopes incarnated in the project, whether due to fault or fallibility, can be uncovered." (cf. Chapter XIII, Core Concepts)(54)

IX Abstract proposal:

A new philosophy of man and humanism, accepted by the Scientific Committee Movement and Cognition-2018 for ORAL presentation for the conference on Movement and Cognition to be held at the Joseph B. Martin Conference Center of Harvard University's School of Medicine in Boston Massachusetts USA between 27-29 July 2018

Keywords: Philosophy, anthropology, domain unto itself, interdisciplinary, reflection

Objective: A new philosophy of man shows that questions about brain, body and cognition are borrowed from the old philosophy, with its focus on ultimate knowledge and the absolute beginning. But we cannot find any answers to these questions if we leave human beings out of the equation. The theoretical basis for the new philosophy was laid by the American philosopher James Joseph Dagenais (1923-1981), who came to the conclusion that philosophical anthropology is not a science, but a domain unto itself, and that a philosophy of man can only come about as a joint undertaking of all sciences, in which the object of study must be man himself. The final explanation of man lies outside all possible scientific views that have ever been formulated, because they lie within the origins of every branch of science, including the science of philosophy. It is the final ground on which the philosophies, of any nature whatsoever, can be practised implicitly or explicitly.

Methods: The methods of a post-modern philosophical anthropology will have to be based on reflection, on the claim that it is possible to debate differences and contrasts on reasonable grounds, and on the individual responsibility for the decisions we all make for ourselves in respect of changes in body and mind. A post-modern version of Sartre's creed: man is and always will be what he makes of himself.

Results: In this sense, human beings as absolute entities have undergone certain developments over millions of years (they have evolved) so that today we can cite a number of features (essential characteristics) in relation to their nature and origin. In this process our empirical involvement can be regarded as the motor that has made us (caused us to develop) into what we are today. This is our everyday reality. We have deduced our essential characteristics (an urge for survival, communication, identity, self-fulfilment, self-determination) from them alone and they can be seen as the motives - which have proved in the course of history to be enduring - for our actions. They therefore do not truly exist, but they apparently typify our most original state of being, set down in billions of cells (matter) that make us who we are.

Conclusion: Whatever meaning the terms brain, body and cognition may have, the foregoing makes it clear that they only take on real significance when they are embedded in the whole of their everyday order of being. This is not the point of the Conference Movement: Brain, Body, Cognition: you regard your hypothesis solely from your own perspective of cognitive neuroscience, without looking at the broader philosophical anthropological implications.

X Explanation New Philosophy of Man & Humanism (53)

1. Old and new philosophy (Rorty (22))

2. The sentiments of philosophers in the 20th century and their call for a systematic philosophical anthropology (Landmann (52))

3. All structure that we ascribe to the world arises from our own observation of it." (Frayn (5))

4. New Philosophy of Man (Dagenais (37)(38), Swaab (5), Lamme (2)(31))

5. Jim Dagenais's definition of philosophical anthropology (37)(38)) and Reinout Bakker's characteristics of philosophical anthropology (3)(33), following in the footsteps of Dagenais
   Philosophy as a basis for a humanist ideology (Van Praag (39)(42)(51))

6. Philosophical anthropology explains how human beings are put together without delving into their cultural characteristics and without moralising (Kant (49), Heidegger (50), Bakker (3)(33))
   Plessner, Scheler and Gehlen (Bakker (3)(33))

7. Core Concepts Philosophical Anthropology
   The absolute entity (Bryson (11))
   Core Concepts: A. Essential (Relative Freedom) B. Relational (Absolute Freedom)
   Summary

1. Old and new philosophy (Rorty (22))

In the 21st century we need a new philosophy as opposed to the old philosophy: a philosophy of man or philosophical anthropology. The importance of a new philosophy of man is that it addresses people all over the world, thus helping us to overcome our differences. And if we look a bit further into the world of the 21st century, we see that the most pressing project will be the search for meaning in the lives of human beings in a globalised world.

Richard Rorty (22) in an interview by Ger Groot in 2007 about philosophy: "Philosophy is a manner of defining ourselves anew, not the gradual discovery of established truths." "In this statement, he showed himself to be a full-blooded American thinker, in the tradition of pragmatists James and Dewey, one who rubbed many of his colleagues the wrong way - in the Anglo-Saxon world because he did not believe that truth could be found through a careful analysis of language and logics, and on the European continent because he refused to speculate on the deep 'mind' that finds truth in its own deepest reflections..... Rorty on the traditional epistemology, the heart of modern philosophy: Questions such as 'what is truth?', 'what is the foundation of our knowledge?' and 'how do our words refer to reality?' have kept Western philosophy on the wrong track for centuries.... Language [he found] is not a reflection of reality, but something that belongs to reality itself. Words work: they achieve certain effects and do not merely obediently process reality into the abstract images in our head that we call 'truth'.... As furious as orthodox philosophers often reacted to Rorty, so intrigued were those who, on both sides of the ocean, had already started to doubt that philosophy should be based on the 'unshakable' foundations which Descartes and many others had sought. In the 1980s and 1990s Rorty thus grew into an original and influential bridge-builder between the more 'metaphysical' European and the 'analytical' Anglo-Saxon way of thought, paradoxically enough by blowing up the mainstays under both traditions."

2. *The sentiments of philosophers in the 20th century and their call for a systematic philosophical anthropology (Landmann (52))*

Michael Landmann (52) very neatly described the sentiments of philosophers in the 20th century and their call for a systematic philosophical anthropology, ultimately to conclude: "Everyone realizes vaguely that the question of man is the question that decides our fate." and "The method of philosophical anthropology is often to start with a noticeable human quality and ask backwards from that: how must a being be constituted if this characteristic fulfils a meaningful and indispensable function in it? In other words, a deduction is made from an observed detail to the presumably still unknown entirety of man." Terms such as reason (Descartes (48)) and empiricism (Kant (49)) are derived from this method, and the terms rationalism and empiricism seem to form a pair of opposites, although they both are related to the same thing, which I have chosen to call 'experience' or 'the process of experience'.

In this context it is striking that scientists and philosophers use all the same words I have used (in respect of perception or cognisance) (feelings, emotions, knowledge, consciousness (Blackmore (5)(13)), mind, soul, will, conscience, etc.) in a fairly random manner, which is quite a frequent practise, and this can only be explained by the fact that these terms more or less overlap; they cannot be defined accurately and are more or less synonymous (because they are based on feeling, on knowing or not knowing) and therefore can all be traced back to the basic terms I use: experience or the process of experience leading to the conclusion or finding.

3. *"All structure that we ascribe to the world arises from our own observation of it" (Frayn (5))*

Statement:
Everything is illusion, nothing is real, we live our lives completely in the (human, illusionist) world of our own creation and reality (fact, realism, God as reality (34)) will always be unknowable to us as human beings. Philosophical anthropology describes this human (illusory) world, of which religion (34) and philosophy, art and culture, science and politics (Karl Popper (15)) are constituent parts. Important in this context: the meaning of language and communication.

English philosopher Michael Frayn (5): "There is no such thing as free will, language proves to be ambiguous and consciousness is still a huge riddle. Even the laws of nature are no more than human artefacts, the product of the way in which we perceive the universe. In short, all structure that we ascribe to the world arises from our own observation of it."

4. *New Philosophy of man (Dagenais (37)(38), Swaab (5), Lamme (2)(31))*

The biggest hurdle in 2500 years of philosophy has always been man himself - more specifically, the contents of his cranium, which a great many words have been used to describe (soul, reason (48), empiricism (49), mind, knowledge, consciousness

(Blackmore (5)(13)), will, and many more). Existentialism and the Phenomenology of Perception (Merleau-Ponty) managed for the first time in the history of mankind to focus philosophy a bit more closely on ourselves. It took us until the end of the 20th century to come to the understanding that "we are our brain" (Dick Swaab (5)) and that "we need to shift our focus from the mind to our brain" (Victor Lamme (2)(31)).

What we then see is 100 billion brain cells, all "chattering with each other" (Victor Lamme (2)(31)), leading us to an initial insight into our history and evolution and our essential characteristics. We discover that our focus is now on processes in the brain, which I have chosen to call 'experience' or 'the process of experience'. The neurological discoveries of the 20th century have not yet resulted in changes to our terminology; we still make use of outdated terms in talking about the new situation.

I have given philosophical anthropology a new concrete substance on the basis of the definition of American philosopher and member of the American Philosophical Association Jim Dagenais (37)(38): "a consistent overall vision of man and his world", so that it can serve as the basis for philosophy and thus as the foundation for human life.

The meaning of basic concepts such as soul, mind, reason, experience, consciousness (Blackmore (5)(13)) and will is completely re-examined. Following developments in the 20th century, traditional definitions no longer serve our purpose; we must rigorously adapt our language to these developments so that it once again meets the basic requirements for communication. Then it allows us to describe a contemporary philosophy of human beings and to find answers to today's questions and issues.

The importance of a new philosophy of man is that it addresses people all over the world, thus helping us to overcome our differences. And if we look a bit further into the world of the 21st century, we see that the most pressing project will be the search for meaning in the lives of human beings in a globalised world. Following the complete existential deconstruction that took place in the 20th century, our confusion on the foundations of our life abounds. The next step, consolidation in the 21st century, has been achieved in my philosophical anthropology.

5. *Jim Dagenais's definition of philosophical anthropology (37)(38)) and Reinout Bakker's characteristics of philosophical anthropology (3)(33), following in the footsteps of Dagenais Philosophy as a basis for a humanist ideology (Van Praag (39)(42)(51))*

Jim Dagenais's definition of philosophical anthropology (37)(38):

"The only claims which philosophy can make to leadership in the total enterprise of understanding man is its capacity to explicitate its own presuppositions ... if the necessary presuppositions of a philosophy of man can be clarified and justified, its claim to be basic can be validated..... The presuppositions of any philosophy, I maintain, involve a fundamental attitude towards myself, the other, and the world. The most fundamental evidence here is that the universe is not a thing, nor even a system of things, not an object or a system of objects, but primordially an interpersonal world, a world of and for persons.

Philosophy can then be defined as a reflection upon the pre-reflexive, pre-philosophical, pre-scientific experiencing of being, that is, upon experiencing before any kind of conscious thematization. If philosophy is a radical and transcendental thinking, that is, a thinking upon the a priori conditions of possibility of all thinking and all experiencing, then the experiencing which is reflected upon must be experiencing in the largest sense. It is the experiencing in my insertion of being - concretely, the experiencing of myself and the other in the world."

Reinout Bakker's characteristics of philosophical anthropology (3)(33), following in the footsteps of Dagenais:

"1. Philosophical anthropology is a domain unto itself, and cannot be replaced by any other anthropology. The final explanation of man lies outside all possible scientific views that have ever been formulated, because they lie within the origins of every branch of science, including the science of philosophy. It is the final ground on which the philosophies, of any nature whatsoever, can be practised implicitly or explicitly.

2. In my inaugural speech of 25 January 1965 I spoke of the necessary collaboration between philosophy and science. Philosophy without contact with the empirical

sciences is empty, but also: the empirical sciences are blind without the contribution of philosophy. If one of these two poles is made absolute, the danger of gross one-sidedness, or even distortion, is imminent. The fact that the ultimate questions about man are so rarely asked stems from giving the scientific foundation of philosophy an absolute status. Many phenomenologists and existentialists have warned against such scientism.

3. The methods of a post-modern philosophical anthropology will have to be based on reflection, on the claim that it is possible to debate differences and contrasts on reasonable grounds, and on the individual responsibility for the decisions we all make for ourselves in respect of changes in body and mind. A post-modern version of Sartre's creed: man is and always will be what he makes of himself."

Philosophy as a basis for a humanist ideology (Van Praag (39)(42)(51))

My philosophical anthropology, as opposed to the ideas of Jaap van Praag (39)(42)(51), presents itself as a basis for a humanist ideology, which makes the prevailing concept in humanist circles, 'humanism without religion' (34), completely obsolete. Although humanism arose in the 20th century out of an anti-religious movement, a humanism without the religions is incomplete, and so it is not entitled to lay claim to that concept, because as an anti-religious movement it can have no independent significance; it is derived from religions, the role of religions within the humanist movement has always led to heated discussions, and agreement has never been reached on this aspect.

6. Philosophical anthropology explains how human beings are put together without delving into their cultural characteristics and without moralising (Kant (49), Heidegger (50), Bakker (3)(33))
Plessner, Scheler and Gehlen (Bakker (3)(33))

All works on philosophical anthropology and humanism published thus far adopt a moralising tone; they give a blueprint for how people should live without going in any depth into how people are put together and how they operate in their dealings with others. Immanuel Kant's 'Anthropologie' (49), published in 1800, already shows this tendency; so does ‘Brief über den Humanismus’ by Martin Heidegger (50) from 1947. In the second half of the 20th century a number of attempts were made to describe philosophical anthropology and humanism, but without lasting results. Moralising continued to predominate, for example in work of Jaap van Praag, Dutch humanist and professor of philosophy at Leiden University (1994, 1958 (39)(42)(51)) and Ad Peperzak, a Dutch professor of philosophy at Loyola University in Chicago, Illinois (1972 and 1975). But a philosophical anthropology must first describe the foundations of human existence without moralising before it can serve as a basis for a humanist life stance.

An exception to this is found in the work of the biological anthropologists Plessner, Scheler and Gehlen, but their findings also earn them the well-considered and conclusive criticism of Reinout Bakker (3)(33): “Reviewing the anthropologists discussed, then we see that biology as an empirical science is an inadequate way of interpreting human beings. The three thinkers leave behind remnants that cannot be divvied up over purely scientific categories.

Plessner centres his anthropology around the eccentricity of human beings, a category that defies empirical investigation. A comparison of humans to animals is not very productive because human beings are always the subject of the comparison” and “Scheler did not see that philosophical anthropology is an integrational philosophical discipline, in which metaphysics must be consistently excommunicated from the mind.

Because it is not useful in a scientific sense the study of man in comparison with animals, prominent in the first half of the 20th century, no longer yields up any meaningful results. The ‘added value’ of man is not expressed in this comparative study. The required empirical method cannot respond to this factor, because it cannot be tested empirically. And how can one in fact start from a comparison between man and animals if the particular character of the actual comparison is not assessed at the same time? If one wishes to demonstrate that man is fundamentally superior to animals, then one must assume that this only can be proved by means of reflections of man on himself, reflections on the basis of which man is aware of himself as an ‘I’ that can study both himself and animals.”

7. *Core Concepts of Philosophical Anthropology*
The absolute entity (Bryson (11))
Core Concepts: A. Essential (Relative Freedom) B. Relational (Absolute Freedom)
Summary

The absolute entity (Bill Bryson: "all life is one" (11))

All life forms can be referred to by this concept. To a greater or lesser degree, they all exhibit its characteristics. Its main characteristics are a common origin, a shared evolution and structure. The common origin and the shared evolution mean that all absolute entities are brought in line with their common origin and are also directly connected to it. Absolute entities are structured so as to be ends in themselves, solely focused on self-fulfilment and therefore fully autonomous. Human beings are therefore also absolute entities, and we will limit our discussion to them.

Core Concepts

A. Essential (Relative Freedom)

The origin and evolution of human beings as absolute entities can be divided into five distinctive segments:

1. Cosmos, which cannot be defined, but which has the following characteristics: Intelligence (Plan, Order, Structure) (34), Energy, Form and Matter
2. Planet Earth and Nature (Laws of Nature)
3. Human Beings: Brain, Male and Female, Reproductive Urge
4. Conception (Insemination), Duality, Birth
5. Unity, Absolute Entity

The defining essential characteristics of human beings as absolute entities are:

1. Dependency and Urge for Survival (Material)
2. Inward-Looking (Closed), Goal in Itself (Autonomy, Being Yourself) (49),

Isolation and Communication (Broad and Immaterial)
3. Identity (Singularity, Character) and Individuality
4. Ultimate Objective: Self-Fulfilment (Development, Search for Meaning)
5. Autonomy (Self-Determination) and Freedom (Relative Freedom)

As absolute entities, human beings operate by means of experience. The concept of experience can be described as parts, or phases, of processes in the brain. These processes are autonomous. Accordingly, experience can be divided into the following parts or phases:

1. Observation (Input) (49)
2. Storage (Memory)
3. Organising (Combining) (49)
4. Conclusion or Finding (Mood, Intuition, Feelings, Emotions, Thought, Knowledge (49), Reason (48), Idea, Mental Grasp, Consciousness (Blackmore (5)(13)), Mind, Soul, Psyche, Will, Conscience, etc.)
5. Plan
6. Performance (Output).

B. Relational (Absolute Freedom)

Communication
Power
The democratic rule of law
Conscience (morals and ethics).

Summary

To summarise, human beings as absolute entities have undergone developments over millions of years (they have evolved) so that today we can point to a number of traits (essential characteristics) in connection with their nature and origin, which we have looked at from a point of view that we generally call empirical reality (the process of experience). In this process our empirical involvement can be regarded as the motor that has made us, or caused us to develop, into what we are today. This is our everyday reality. This alone has given us our essential characteristics (urge for survival, communication, identity, self-fulfilment, self-determination), and these essential characteristics can be seen as the motives - which have proved in the course of history to be enduring - for our actions. This implies that they do not truly exist, but they apparently typify our most original state of being, set down in billions of cells (matter) that make us who we are.

It follows from the nature of human beings as absolute entities that the way in which they get along with each other is primarily determined by the free interplay of forces. They can impose limitations (self-limitations, voluntarily) on themselves for the sake of peace (conscience) and can avail themselves of norms (rules of morals and decency) as guidelines for their actions. This involves the relationships between individuals in contrast to individuals in a group (family and friends, clubs, companies, religious communities, government) where the group imposes norms (rules of morals and decency, mores, customs and usages, laws) on its participants, who must adhere to them.

We can thus conclude that the free interplay of forces (absolute freedom) is inherent in human nature, that any limitation of this is alien to human nature and that the use of norms is only prompted by a need for ordering, depending on the circumstances (efficiency), when there is a clash of interests. This absolute freedom in connection with the realisation of the total of all essential characteristics of human beings as absolute entities in relation to others must be distinguished from the relative freedom of people in realising their autonomy in the form of self-determination, which is limited in this sense.

XI Summary New Philosophy of Man & Humanism

1. Old and new philosophy

In the 21st century we need a new philosophy as opposed to the old philosophy: a philosophy of man or philosophical anthropology. The importance of a new philosophy of man is that it addresses people all over the world, thus helping us to overcome our differences. And if we look a bit further into the world of the 21st century, we see that the most pressing project will be the search for meaning in the lives of human beings in a globalised world.

The theoretical basis for the new philosophy was laid by American philosopher and member of the American Philosophical Association James Joseph Dagenais (1923-1981) (37)(38), who came to the conclusion that philosophical anthropology is not a science, but a domain unto itself and cannot be replaced by any other anthropology. The final explanation of man lies outside all possible scientific views that have ever been formulated, because they lie within the origins of every branch of science, including the science of philosophy. It is the final ground on which the philosophies, of any nature whatsoever, can be practised implicitly or explicitly.

Dutch humanist Jaap van Praag (1911-1981) (39)(42)(51) and Dutch philosopher Reinout Bakker (1920-1987) (3)(33) elaborated on the findings of Dagenais, Van Praag for humanism and Bakker for the philosophy of man or philosophical anthropology. Taking this one step further, the new philosophy of man can serve as the basis for a humanist ideology.

In his inaugural speech of 25 January 1965 Bakker spoke of the necessary collaboration between philosophy and science. Philosophy without contact with the empirical sciences is empty, but also: the empirical sciences are blind without the contribution of philosophy. If one of these two poles is made absolute, the danger of gross one-sidedness, or even distortion, is imminent. The fact that the ultimate questions about man are so rarely asked stems from giving the scientific foundation of philosophy an absolute status. Many phenomenologists and existentialists have warned against such scientism.

The methods of a post-modern philosophical anthropology will have to be based on reflection, on the claim that it is possible to debate differences and contrasts on reasonable grounds, and on the individual responsibility for the decisions we all make for ourselves in respect of changes in body and mind. A post-modern version of Sartre's creed: man is and always will be what he makes of himself.

2. New Philosophy of man (Dagenais (37)(38)), Swaab (5)), Lamme (2)(31))

The biggest hurdle in 2500 years of philosophy has always been man himself - more specifically, the contents of his cranium, which a great many words have been used to describe (reason (Descartes (48)), empiricism (Kant (49)), mind, knowledge, consciousness (Blackmore (5)(13)), and many more). Existentialism and the Phenomenology of Perception (Merleau-Ponty) managed for the first time in the history of mankind to focus philosophy a bit more closely on ourselves. It took us until the end of the 20th century to come to the understanding that "we are our brain" (Dick Swaab (5)) and that "we need to shift our focus from the mind to our brain"(Victor Lamme (2)(31)).

What we then see is 100 billion brain cells, all "chattering with each other" (Victor Lamme (2)(31)), leading us to an initial insight into our history and evolution and our essential characteristics. We discover that our focus is now on processes in the brain, which I have chosen to call 'experience' or 'the process of experience'. The neurological discoveries of the 20th century have not yet resulted in changes to our terminology; we still make use of outdated terms in talking about the new situation.

I have given philosophical anthropology a new concrete substance on the basis of the definition of American philosopher Jim Dagenais (37)(38): "a consistent overall vision of man and his world", so that it can serve as the basis for philosophy and thus as the foundation for human life.

The meaning of basic concepts such as mind, reason, experience, consciousness (Blackmore (5)(13)) and will is completely re-examined. Following developments in the 20th century, traditional definitions no longer serve our purpose; we must rigorously adapt our language to these developments so that it once again meets the basic requirements for communication. Then it allows us to describe a contemporary philosophy of human beings and to find answers to today's questions and issues.

Following the complete existential deconstruction that took place in the 20th century, our confusion on the foundations of our life abounds. The next step, consolidation in the 21st century, has been achieved in my philosophical anthropology.

XII Notes

(1) Van de Vall R., 1994, *Een subliem gevoel van plaats, Een filosofische interpretatie van het werk van Barnett Newman*, Historische Uitgeverij; Baumeister Th., 2001, *De Filosofie en de Kunsten, van Plato tot Beuys*, Damon, ISBN 90 5573 0173.

This is in contrast with Hugh Honour and John Fleming, 2009, 7th revised edition, *A World History of Art*, Laurence King Publishing, ISBN 978-1-85669-579-4 and ISBN 978-1-85669-584-8, who qualify Newman's *Vir Heroicus Sublimis as* "... reducing pictorial language to its basic elements ..." and ask in general about his works of art: "... though whether they can bear the weight of meaning their titles sometimes suggest may be doubted".

(2) Buytendijk F.J.J., 1965, *Prolegomena van een Antropologische Fysiologie*, Aula-Boeken Utrecht Antwerpen, Het Spectrum, intended for the fields of medicine and psychology, who is of the opinion that "the psycho-physical problem cannot be solved empirically".

Barendregt H.P., 2007, Professor of Foundations of Mathematics and Information Science, Radboud University, on *Modellen van het Bewustzijn* in NRC.next of 6 February (www.nrcnext.nl).

Lamme, V.A.F., 2007 Professor of Cognitive Neurosciences, University of Amsterdam, on "the neurobiological foundation of consciousness" in *NRC Handelsblad* of 16 October 2007 (www.nrc.nl), interview by Marion de Boo [Bewust heen en weer praten]: "The more we understand about this subject, the more abstruse becomes the problem of mind-body separation."

Achterhuis H.J., 2008, *Met alle geweld, Een filosofische zoektocht*, Lemniscaat, ISBN 978 90 477 0127 9 or ISBN 978 90 477 0120 0.

Philipse H., 2007, *Atheïstisch manifest en de onredelijkheid van religie, Met een voorwoord van Ayaan Hirsi Ali*, Uitgeverij Bert Bakker Amsterdam, ISBN 978 90 351 26541.

(3) Bakker R., 1981, *Wijsgerige Antropologie van de Twintigste Eeuw*, Van Gorcum, Assen, Terreinverkenningen in de Filosofie, ISBN 90 232 1800 0.

Peperzak A., 1972/1975, Professor of Philosophy, Loyola University, Chicago, Illinois, in his *Inleidingen Wijsgerige Antropologie I en II entitled Vrijheid and U en ik*, published by Ambo Bilthoven, ISBN 90 263 0195 2 and 90 263 2008 6, with the following text on the back of the first volume: "There is no good manual of philosophical anthropology, which is strange for a field in which so many original studies have been published and which basks in such great interest. Ad Peperzak makes an attempt to fill this void."

Achterhuis H.J., *ibid.*, note (2).

Philipse H., *ibid.*, note (2).

Hampden-Turner C., 1970, Radical Man, *The Process of Psycho-Social Developmen*t, Schenkman Publishing Company, Massachusetts, not only for his urgent call for "… a new philosophy for the social sciences - a complete reassessment of what a science of humanity should be", but also for his supporting role in the writing of *Models of Man* by Jim Dagenais (38).

(4) Cf. the conclusions from the climate change conference in Bangkok of May 2007, where an urgent call was made for the need for a "new way of life" and "changes in … consumption patterns".

Cf. the appeal by Chinese premier Wen Jiabao to the National People's Congress in March 2008 for "new forms of thought" and "breaking with the traditional, established patterns of thought" in NRC Handelsblad of Saturday 15 March and Sunday 16 March 2007 (www.nrc.nl): *Zwijgen geen optie meer voor China*, Tibet (cont. from p. 1).

Indian scientist Rajendra Pachauri, chairman of the Intergovernmental Panel on Climate Change (IPCC), the UN climate panel, in NRC Handelsblad (Economie) of Monday 1 September 2008 (www.nrc.nl) [*Minder vlees beperkt uitstoot*] on cattle breeding as a cause of the greenhouse effect: “A change in life style and consumption patterns is badly needed” (Interview by Hans van der Lugt).

Robert Zoellick, President of the World Bank, in NRC Handelsblad (Opinie) of Tuesday 14 October 2008 (www.nrc.nl) [*India, Brazilië en China moeten G7 bijstaan*], “Group of industrial powers is not big enough to resolve today’s problems..... The financial crisis offers an opportunity for a new multilateral network. Rising powers want to be heard too..... We should consider setting up a new steering committee, one that includes Brazil, China, India, Mexico, Russia, Saudi Arabia, South Africa and the present G7, that holds regular meetings, with active formal and informal discussions. The group should not simply replace the G7 by another group of countries, but must be continually adjusted to the circumstances. We cannot use methods from the ‘old’ world to create the new one.....”

(5) Blackmore S.J., 2005, Professor of Psychology at the University of Plymouth, *Consciousness, A Very Short Introduction*, Oxford University Press, Great Clarendon Street, Oxford OX2 6DP, ISBN 13: 978-0-19-280585-0 and 0-19-280585-1 and in NRC Handelsblad of 7 December 2006 (www.nrc.nl): [*Er bestaat alleen ervaring, vergeet de rest*] on the illusion of consciousness and taking leave of the Self, who has given up the idea that she has a free will and a Self: “Consciousness is a story told in retrospect” (discussion and interview by Hendrik Spiering).

Blackmore S.J., 2009, *Ten Zen Questions*, published by One World Publications, Oxford, ISBN 978-1-85168-642-1

Blackmore S.J., 2011, *Zen and the Art of Consciousness*, published by One World Publications, Oxford, 2011, ISBN 978-1-85168-798-5:

“Almost all scientists and most philosophers claim to be materialists (or at least not to be dualists). In other words, they ought to assume that the brain process would start the action, and not be at all surprised by the results. Yet they were surprised, and go on being surprised. I think the reason is that they, like most people, *feel* as though they consciously decide to act, and that their consciousness causes things to happen.

So here we have a simple clash between the physical and the mental; between how things are in the physical brain and how they feel from the inside. How do we resolve it?

I suspect that we will never do so without a revolution in the way we think about consciousness. I don't mean a revolution involving quantum physics, or telepathy, or new forces of nature, or other-worldly spirits and souls. I mean a revolution that goes deep down into our own minds and actually transforms our experience, so that we can talk and think in a different way. And this way would have to be something so counter-intuitive that it really does root out dualism … no-one has yet found a special place where consciousness happens, or a special process uniquely correlated with conscious, as opposed to unconscious, events." (see also note (13)).

Frayn M., 2006, *The Human Touch, Our Part in the Creation of a Universe*, Faber Books, ISBN 978-0-571-23217-8 and 978-0-571-23217-5: "There is no such thing as free will (brain study has shown that a decision has already been taken half a second before we become aware of it), language proves to be ambiguous and consciousness ... is still a huge riddle. Even the laws of nature are no more than human artefacts, the product of the way in which we perceive the universe. In short, all structure that we ascribe to the world arises from our own observation of it." (book review by Rob van den Berg in NRC Handelsblad of 8 December 2006 (www.nrc.nl) [*Het heelal zit in ons hoofd, Zin en onzin over mens, aarde en kosmos*]).

Watson P., 2005, *Ideas: A History from Fire to Freud*, Phoenix, Orion Books Ltd., London, ISBN 978-0-7538-2089-6, p. 1015, who asks himself whether "…the essential Platonic notion of the 'inner self' is misconceived?" only to conclude: "There is no inner self … because there is nothing to find." He states that "the general view [is] that the self arises in some way from brain activity - from the action of electrons" and is surprised that we "still don't know even how to talk about consciousness, about the self."

Van Gijn J., 2007, speaking about his farewell speech on the relationship of body to mind [*De ongrijpbare geest*], in which he called the psyche "an impalpable brain activity", remarking: "… we know for sure that the psyche - the mind - ultimately consists in the operation of cells, connections, molecules and electric currents. But it is such a huge network that we will need several generations of information technology to gain even the slightest grasp of it ... so for the time being it is impalpable", interview by Wim Köhler NRC Handelsblad 9 and 10 June 2007 (www.nrc.nl).

Swaab D.F., 2008, emeritus professor of neurobiology at the University of Amsterdam, also founder of the Netherlands Brain Bank (for worldwide scientific study of the brain), a division of the Netherlands Institute for Neurosciences of the Royal Dutch Academy of Sciences in Amsterdam, in NRC Handelsblad Zaterdag&cetera of Saturday 22 March & Sunday 23 March 2008 (www.nrc.nl) [*Wij zijn ons brein*]: "Free will is an illusion. It is not we, but the brain, that determines. Our character, personality, our sexual orientation and what we refer to as mind, it is all found in the brain ... a person ... is his brain....." Saturday 30 August & Sunday 31 August 2008 (www.nrc.nl) [*De 21 gram*]: "There is no such thing as the soul. When we die, 100 billion brain cells cease working."

Swaab D.F., 2014, *We Are Our Brains: From the Womb to Alzheimer's*, Allen Lane, 0844 871 15 15, ISBN 978-0812992960.

Stone H. and Stone S., 1989, *Embracing Our Selves, The Voice Dialogue Manual*, Nataraj Publishing, a division of New World Library, 14 Pamaron Way, Novato, CA 94949, V.S., ISBN 1-882591-06-2, on the nature of consciousness (p. 18): "In approaching the definition of consciousness, we start with the basic idea that consciousness is not an entity - it is a process. What we will be defining, therefore, is not consciousness but the evolution of consciousness. We call it consciousness, but we are not talking about a static condition of being. As far as we are concerned, people do not become conscious; consciousness is not a state that people strive to attain. Consciousness is a process that must be lived out - an evolutionary process that continually changes from one moment to the next." (www.voicedialogueinternational.com).

Yalom I.D., 2009, emeritus professor of psychiatry at Stanford University, Stanford, California and existential psychotherapist, *Staring at the Sun: Overcoming the Terror of Death*, Published by Jossey-Bass, 989 Market Street, San Francisco, CA 94103-1741 – www.josseybass.com, ISBN 978-0-7879-9668-0 (cloth) and ISBN 978-0-470-40181-1 (paperback), who uses the term "awakening experience" alongside the term "awakening consciousness" and assumes "deep structures of existence or, to use the theologian Paul Tillich's felicitous term, *ultimate concerns*: death, isolation, meaning in life and freedom", comparable with my concepts of experience and essential characteristics of human beings as absolute entities. The four ultimate concerns named form the backbone of his manual from 1980, *Existential Psychotherapy*, in which he gives a detailed description of phenomenology and the therapeutic implications of each.

(6) Roothaan A.C.M., 2005, *Terugkeer van de Natuur, De betekenis van natuurervaring voor een nieuwe ethiek*, Uitgeverij Klement, Kampen, ISBN 90 77070 71 0.

Cliteur P., 2005, in his dissertation *Natuurrecht Cultuurrecht Conservatisme*, Universitaire Pers Fryslân Acta Launiana under the auspices of the Rudolf von Laun Institute for Applied Metaphysics, ISBN 90 5573 663 5.

Watson P., ibid., note (5), who presumes that the solution to the problem he has identified lies outside ourselves: "We human beings are part of nature and therefore we are more likely to find out about our 'inner' nature, to understand ourselves, by looking outside ourselves, at our role and place as animals." He presumes that the next step will be found in the hard sciences: "The natural sciences have proved to be a huge success with regard to the world outside of human beings, the Aristotelian world....."

Philipse H., ibid., note (2).

(7) Van Efferen P., 1998, MD, *Modern Medisch woordenboek*, praktische snelzoekgids van A - Z, Uitgeverij Elmar b.v., Rijswijk, ISBN 90389 02921.

See also *Het grote medische handboek, met medicijnenindex* (under the auspices of the Health Council, London, Medical Faculty, Vrije Universiteit, Brussels, Dutch Ministry of Health, Welfare Sport, The Hague, National Institutes of Health, Bethesda, MD (USA) and the World Health Organization (WHO), Geneva, compiled by an international team of respected physicians and researchers), Rebo Productions, 2009, ISBN 978- 90-366-2651-4, in particular De mens, pp. 9-83, where the following quotation is taken from the chapter entitled Het mysterie mens:

"Signals and potentials (pp. 10-11)

Every object is surrounded by an observable aura: it reflects light, it makes a sound or it vaporises or sublimates: that is, it emits substances to the surroundings.

Because of this, an object can be seen, heard or smelled at a distance. Images, sounds or smells, however, are not the object itself, but very weak energies that emanate from the object and can stimulate the highly perceptive senses. We call such stimuli signals. They are converted by the senses into electrical potentials that are conducted to the nervous system, where they are inhibited or strengthened, can be separated or combined and are then distributed via the nerves that operate the muscles. The muscles thus receive a signal prompting them to contract and the body is set in motion.
In this final phase we see the discharge of a high-energy system (the muscle). The low-energy system acts as a spark generator: it is the fuse in the tinderbox.
We can regard these signals as a code or language in which reality speaks. The code is converted in our senses, or translated into another code, one that is more like our Morse code. In our brain, this code is again transformed in a way that we can call interpretation. Interpretation is a mental process.
Generally speaking, the nervous system learns to interpret through experience. In the animal kingdom too, most requisite knowledge is customarily acquired in childhood. In animals and humans, this learning process is slow and defective.
The nervous system is always spontaneous and hard-working - it produces fantasies and dreams - but it seems to have difficulty with learning. Even so, some people keep going for almost a century, in the hope that they will be buried fully knowing all there is to know."

"Socialisation (pp. 12-13)

The last source of conflicts is found in the social hierarchy. History has taught us that it is easier for people, as subjects, to obey good rulers than it is for rulers to be good for their subjects. The answer of evolution to the imminent conflict situation in which human beings find themselves is socialisation.
Socialisation is brought about by the organ that regulates the behaviour of human beings in the world and in their group: the nervous system. In order to carry out this very onerous task, the nervous system has grown into an organ far exceeding that of the other animals in volume and capacity.
This process is called cephalisation. It is characteristic of the evolution of primates

and it has gone even further in human evolution. It has made human beings the most complicated mechanism known in the universe. In cephalisation, nature has made a choice between aggression and socialisation, opting for the latter. Repression means mitigating aggression in favour of socialisation. How does the brain bring about repression? Animal behaviour is guided by the signals it receives. This guidance may have a semblance of providence, but it is simply the processing of experiences that have regularly repeated themselves.
Animal behaviour has an average efficiency that does not rule out catastrophes, but as a rule it is satisfactory. Human behaviour is also guided by signals. To the signals emitted by nature, human beings have added signals of their own invention: symbols. Our language is a system of symbols, by which we can guide our behaviour in the group. Some of our symbols do not describe our given reality, but set standards for future behaviour.
We call these symbols values. Signals and special signals, symbols and special symbols, values, guide our behaviour. When we drive a car, we are guided by signals - for example, the edge of the road, a symbol, and for example by a traffic sign, representing a value: thou shalt not kill. In itself, the world of symbols is not neutral. Because we possess it, we are smarter than animals.
But the world of values is imperative. Because they possess it, human beings are elevated above other kingdoms of organisms."

(8) *Coëlho Zakwoordenboek der Geneeskunde*, 26ste geheel herziene druk, Elsevier - PBNA, Arnhem - 2000 ISBN 90 6228 322 5.

Zakwoordenboek van de Psychiatrie, Derde druk, Elsevier - Arnhem - 2001 ISBN 90 6228 366 7.

Cf. *Psychoanalytisch woordenboek, Begrippen, Termen, Personen, Literatuur,* Derde Herziene & Vermeerderde Editie, Boom, 2008, ISBN 978 90 8506 614 0; this dictionary has an accompanying website, www.psychoanalytischwoordenboek.nl.

Klukhuhn A., 2007, for a comprehensive study of contemporary views on the nature, significance and origin, particularly of the words consciousness, free will and body and mind, *De geschiedenis van het denken, filosofie, wetenschap, kunst en cultuur van de oudheid tot nu*, Uitgeverij Bert Bakker Amsterdam, zevende druk 2007, ISBN

978 90 351 3176 7, specifically chapter II, Hersenen en bewustzijn, pp. 127-176 and the notes, pp. 590-598. He remarks as follows on scientific research of consciousness (p. 142): "All the better that despite all those pitfalls, scientific researchers have dared to make that troublesome subject of consciousness ... the subject of study. But it has not been for long, because thirty years ago it was still customary for psychologists to resolve the problem of consciousness by deeming it unimportant or unwanted in the study of human behaviour, or worse yet, by denying that such a thing as consciousness existed. But although nowadays techniques have been developed by which the brain can be studied while it is in full operation ... the question remains whether this will lead to greater understanding of the how and why of consciousness." On the debate between the mechanists and the vitalists (pp. 151-152): "The fact that this is no longer conducted is simply because, on account of the lengthy and fruitless trench warfare, people have lost interest in it. And the same will undoubtedly be the case with the debate on consciousness....."

In this context it is striking that Klukhuhn uses all the same words I have used (in respect of perception or cognisance) (feelings, emotions, knowledge, consciousness, mind, soul, will, conscience, etc.) throughout his work in a fairly random manner, which is quite a frequent practice, and this can only be explained by the fact that these terms more or less overlap; they cannot be defined accurately and are more or less synonymous (because they are based on feeling, on knowing or not knowing) and therefore can all be traced back to the basic terms I use: experience or the process of experience leading to the conclusion or finding.

For recent studies on consciousness and unconsciousness, see:

Dijksterhuis A., 2007, Professor of Psychology of the Subconscious at Radboud University, *Het slimme onbewuste, Denken met gevoel*, Uitgeverij Bert Bakker Amsterdam ISBN 978 90 351 2968 9, who reduces consciousness to the end product of unconsciousness, by which, apart from the confusion of terms, the problems are merely displaced.

Van Lommel P., 2007, *Eindeloos bewustzijn, Een wetenschappelijke visie op de bijna-doodervaring*, Uitgeverij Ten Have, ISBN 978 90 259 5778 0 and an interview by Wilma de Rek in the column Het Vervolg in De Volkskrant of Saturday 10 November 2007 (www.vk.nl), p. 22, [Aan alles komt geen eind], who says that "… expanded consciousness cannot be localised at a certain time and place. Consciousness is non-local, it is everywhere….. The brain does not produce consciousness, it only facilitates it; it ensures that you can experience part of your consciousness as 'waking consciousness' … I think that your consciousness comes in contact with the physical at the time of conception."

Van Peursen C.A., 1994, for a comprehensive (historic) overview and discussion of the confusing, well-nigh inaccessible body-mind problem, *Lichaam-Ziel-Geest, Inleiding tot een Wijsgerige Antropologie*, Bijleveld Utrecht, Negende druk 1994, ISBN 9061316448.

(9) Mielke J., Konigsberg L., Relethford J., 2006, *Human Biological Variation*, Oxford University Press (www.oup.com), ISBN 0-19-518871-3.

(10) Rob van den Berg, ibid., note (5):

"*String theory* tries to build a bridge between Einstein's theory of relativity and the quantum theory and it is the most important candidate for a 'theory of everything': an overarching description of nature at a basic level. It does not work with elementary particles such as electrons and quarks, but something more resembling minuscule elastic strings that can oscillate in different ways."

(11) Bryson B., 2005, *A Short History of Nearly Everything*, Doubleday, London, ISBN 0385 609612 (p. 517): "It can all begin to seem impossibly complicated, and in some ways it is impossible complicated. But there is an underlying simplicity in all this, too, owing to an equally elemental underlying unity in the way life works. All the tiny, deft chemical processes that animate cells … evolved just once and have stayed pretty well fixed ever since across the whole of nature.

Every living thing is an elaboration on a single original plan. As humans we are mere increments – each of us a musty archive of adjustments, adaptations, modifications and providential tinkering stretching back 3.8 billion years. Remarkably, we are even quite closely related to fruit and vegetables. About half the chemical functions that take place in a banana are fundamentally the same as the chemical functions that take place in you. *It cannot be said too often:* ***all life is one*** [emphasis added by author].

That is, and I suspect will ever prove to be, the most profound true statement there is."

(12) Ten Kate L., 2007, Encyclopedie van de *Filosofie, Van de Oudheid tot vandaag*, redactie Rebekka Bremmer, Laurens ten Kate en Eelke Warrink, Uitgeverij Boom Amsterdam, ISBN 978 90 8506 457 2, (p. 152):

"Experience

In general: all knowledge that is not acquired outright, but that goes together with consciousness. Different concepts of experience have been developed in philosophy:

1 experience as a sensory perception and observation (also called empiricism) in empiricism, positivism and logical positivism

2 the dynamic process by which consciousness (which must be understood to mean every relationship between subject and object) becomes aware, or conscious, of its object.

This concept of experience was chiefly put forward by Hegel in *The Phenomenology of Spirit*. In the twentieth century many subject-critical thinkers such as Benjamin, Bataille and Nancy translated the dynamic concept of experience into a concept describing the process of undergoing events and emotions. In the process of experience, the subject was said to lose a certain degree of self-control, and therefore to lose his subjectivity as an autonomous and thus to lose consciousness.

On this point the distinction between Erlebnis and Erfahrung plays a role in modern philosophical traditions. Primarily in nineteenth and twentieth century hermeneutics, but also in Benjamin's work, Erlebnis is seen as an isolated experience a person has (whereby the subject remains intact), while Erfahrung stands for the continual and cumulative experience undergone by a person. Erfahrung is dynamic in that the experiencing subject becomes involved in an event of giving meaning or losing meaning, which shifts the horizon of the actual experience.

Bataille's concept of a sovereign inner experience (as elaborated in his *L'expérience intérieure*) is a further radicalisation of this hermeneutic concept of Erfahrung: the sovereignty of experience consists precisely in a loss of self that is at the same time impossible (until one dies).

Experience as a source of knowledge

Experience as a source of knowledge is often contrasted with reason. Philosophy often works with the contrast between empiricism, where experience alone is the source of knowledge, and rationalism, in which reason is regarded as the chief source of knowledge. However, the contrast between reason and experience is relative. This is evident when we realise that we only have knowledge of our reason because we perceive ourselves as beings endowed with reason.

In science too, we see an interaction between reason and experience. In an empirical field such as that covered by the natural sciences, experience in the sense of sensory perception indeed plays a decisive role, but experience is guided by reason. Our intellect determines what experiences are important and therefore what observations or experiments are needed to gain these experiences.

Other empirical sciences, such as psychology, sociology and history, work with the interaction between reason and experience. Particularly since the rise of empirical sciences, how much of their interaction is based on reason and how much on experience has been the subject of much philosophical discussion.

Kant in particular was deeply involved with this issue. He assumed that experience was indispensable for obtaining knowledge, but also stated that design and systematisation, which alone lead to true knowledge, arise from forms of knowledge inherent to human beings which are therefore invariable. Although later the significance of different forms of knowledge was generally recognised, the forms were regarded as rather freely chosen models.

Bataille G., 1989, *Inner experience*, (original French edition 1943)

Freudiger J., Petrus K., 1996, (eds.) *Der Begriff der Erfahrung in der Philosophie des 20. Jahrhunderts*.

Langbehn C., 2005, *Metaphysik der Erfahrung. Zur Grundlegung einer Philosophie der Rechtfertigung beim frühen Nietzsche.*

Nancy J.-L., 1993, *The Experience of Freedom* (original edition 1988)"

(13) Blackmore S.J., ibid., note (5), *Ten Zen Questions and Zen and the Art of Consciousness*, in reply to the question whether anyone will ever be able to point out a place "where consciousness happens": "Many neuroscientists think so, and are hunting for the 'neural correlates of consciousness' to find it. They are looking for a certain part of the brain, or a particular process, which reliably correlates with conscious as opposed to unconscious processes. This is something of a Holy Grail for consciousness studies. But if I don't know which sights and sounds I was conscious of, and which I was not, and I cannot tell anyone else which I was conscious of, then no one can possibly know, and so this whole line of scientific research must be entirely misguided."

Van Lommel P., ibid., note (8) "... more than ninety percent of neuroscientists accept the hypothesis [that] consciousness is located in the brain".

(14) Bryson B., ibid., note (11) (p. 513): "All organisms are in some sense slaves to their genes. That's why salmon and spiders and other types of creatures more or less beyond counting are prepared to die in the process of mating. The desire to breed, to disperse one's genes, is the most powerful impulse in nature. As Sherwin B. Nuland has put it: 'Empires fall, ids explode, great symphonies are written, and behind all of it is a single instinct that demands satisfaction.' From an evolutionary point of view, sex is really just a reward mechanism to encourage us to pass on our genetic material."

(15) Bor J., Petersma E. (ed.), 2000, *De verbeelding van het denken, Geïllustreerde geschiedenis van de westerse en oosterse filosofie*, Beeldredactie Jelle Kingma, Uitgeverij Contact, Amsterdam/Antwerpen, zesde druk oktober 2000, ISBN 90 254 1398-6, with articles by Dr. Th. De Boer, Dr. G. Chemparathy, Dr. R. Fontaine, Prof. E. van Leeuwen, C. Offermans, Prof. H. Philipse, Prof. L.M. de Rijk, Prof. A.J. Vanderjagt, Prof. C. Verhoeven, Prof. H. Visser, Prof. S. IJsseling, Prof. E. Zürcher and with assistance from Dr. C. Anbeek, Dr. S.C.A. Drieman and Dr. L. Ramaker, *particularly on the significance of the imagination for philosophy, which is considered to be of analogous application to "science and technology, art and religion" in the introduction (p. 9)*

and the epilogue (p. 383).

Popper K., 1945, (1902-1994) on the significance of imagination for science, later elaborated for politics in *The Open Society and its Enemies*.

(16) Swaab D.F., note (5), in NRC Handelsblad Zaterdag& cetera of Saturday 4 October & Sunday 5 October 2008 (www.nrc.nl), p. 19 [*Geen keus*]: "Homosexuality cannot be cured. Not by prayer, not by electroshocks and not by emetic therapy..... Everything points in the direction of early programming of our sexual orientation in the womb, by which it is established for the rest of our life..... Until recently homosexuality was regarded as an illness by the medical profession as well. Not until 1992 was homosexuality removed from the ICD-10 (International Classification of Diseases)."

(17) Barber B.R., 2007, American political scientist on consumerism, the manipulative nature and all-controlling influence of advertising and the magnitude of advertising budgets in the world and in the United States in particular, *Consumed: How Markets Corrupt Children, Infantilize Adults, and Swallow Citizens Whole*, originally published by W.W. Norton & Company in NRC Handelsblad, Opinie & Debat, pp. 15 and 16, of Saturday 15 and Sunday 16 September 2007 (www.nrc.nl) [*De infantilisering van de consument is een bedreiging van de democratie*:

"More and more adults become infantilised. Consumption is on its way to becoming the highest, often the only, ideal. This results in a new cultural norm from which is difficult to escape and which has far-reaching political consequences: consumers are not citizens; commercialism has made us less free as citizens."

Lindstrom M., Van de Velde P., 2009, *Buyology*, on "... neuromarketing, in which results from brain research are used to determine advertising strategies." (Interview in De Financiële Telegraaf of Saturday 14 March 2009 (www.telegraaf.nl), p. T20 [*Spiegel neuronen sturen onze kooplust: Marketinggoeroe doet boekje open*].

(18) Pachauri R., ibid., note (4): "In democracies, change only takes place when it is truly wanted by people. If people realise the consequences of their present lifestyle, they will want change. But this awareness must come from the people themselves. Politicians will respond accordingly."

(19) On the magnitude and seriousness of the problems, see NRC Handelsblad Wetenschap of Thursday 25 September 2008 (www.nrc.nl) [*Uitstoot van CO2 stijgt razendsnel*]: "Worldwide emissions of greenhouse gas CO2 are rising faster than predicted in the least favourable scenario. Since 2000, carbon dioxide emissions have grown four times as rapidly as in the previous decade." The main editorial of Friday 26 September 2008 (www.nrc.nl): "The climate issue requires a more rapid response. Although spending reductions can help, it is more courageous and more effective if stricter standards are set right now for energy production and industrial production." (For more information, see www.globalcarbonproject.org)

(20) *It is uncertain whether votes cast in recent decades were actually valid, since the government has decided against any further use of the voting machines, designating "the paper ballot and genuine ballot box the only reliable manner of voting", because the Amsterdam preliminary relief judge and two committees of eminent statesmen determined that approval had erroneously been granted to the Nedap voting machine used in the elections of November 2006 and March 2007.*

One of these committees in April 2007:

"The minister is unable to set standards and does not know how the machines work or how inspections are held. Holding a recount as a control mechanism was held to be unnecessary. There are no rules for storage, transport and security of voting machines."

NRC Handelsblad of 28 September 2007 (www.nrc.nl):

"Since the Home Ministry decided to define standards for the reliability and security of voting machines, the Nedap machines have proved to meet not a single one. Even completely rebuilding them will not bring a solution .....

One year ago the pressure group against voting machines (wijvertrouwenstemcomputersniet.nl) showed that the voting machines made by Nedap - which is the sole manufacturer of voting machines in the Netherlands - could very simply be hacked and that once cast, votes could be "tapped". (From the editorial page: "The ministry simply gave away control. Officials gave the manufacturer a free hand despite the many well-known defects. Because today's voting machines are unfit, we have to go back to using pencils. How an 'inalienable core responsibility of government' was relinquished".)

Finally: "... voting procedures are at the heart of the democratic system ... it has been demonstrated that the voting computers used by the Home Ministry leaked information, thus breaching the constitutional right to vote by secret ballot ... the minister had inadequate control of elections ... Nedap had improper influence on sensitive procedures in relation to ballot boxes ... the Lower House must take action so that it can be established who was responsible for these mistakes and what consequences should be attached to this, because the voting procedure is and remains pre-eminently a matter of trust; after voting, voters must feel certain that their votes actually count and that elections are not rigged ..." (editorial, p. 9).

It makes one wonder as to the foundation of the mandate given to the government and the Lower House and if there should prove to be no basis for this decision, whether it should have led to early elections and the objectives of the government organisation reviewed.

(21) Van Gijn J., ibid., note (5)

(22) Rorty R., 2007, Professor of Comparative Literature at Stanford University in California in an article by Ger Groot in NRC Handelsblad of 11 June 2007 (www.nrc.nl): "'Philosophy is a manner of defining ourselves anew, not the gradual discovery of established truths.' In this statement, he showed himself to be a full-blooded American thinker, in the tradition of pragmatists James and Dewey, one who rubbed many of his colleagues the wrong way – in the Anglo-Saxon world because he did not believe that truth could be found through a careful analysis of language and logics, and on the European continent because he refused to speculate on the deep 'mind' that finds truth in its own deepest reflections..... Rorty on the traditional epistemology, the heart of modern philosophy: Questions such as 'what is truth?', 'what is the foundation of our knowledge?' and 'how do our words refer to reality?' have kept western philosophy on the wrong track for centuries.... Language [he found] is not a reflection of reality, but something that belongs to reality itself. Words work: they achieve certain effects and do not merely obediently process reality into the abstract images in our head that we call 'truth'..... As furious as orthodox philosophers often reacted

to Rorty, so intrigued were those who, on both sides of the ocean, had already started to doubt that philosophy should be based on the 'unshakable' foundations which Descartes and many others had sought. In the 1980s and 1990s Rorty thus grew into an original and influential bridge-builder between the more 'metaphysical' European and the 'analytical' Anglo-Saxon way of thought, paradoxically enough by blowing up the mainstays under both traditions."

Bor J., ibid. note (15) in his epilogue to *De verbeelding van het denken*, who starts out with the words: "With Rorty, an end came to the tale of philosophy told here", and then proceeds to set forth the state of affairs and reflect on the future of philosophy.

(23) Hellinger B., *Zweierlei Glück*, Carl-Auer-Systeme Verlag, Heidelberg;

English translation: *Love's Hidden Symmetry*, Zeig, Tucker & Co., Phoenix, Arizona, USA.

Hellinger B., *Der grosse Konflikt, die Antwort*, Goldmann Verlag a division of Verlagsgruppe Random House GmbH, München, Germany.

(24) Terpstra G.A., 2008, Conquest of Abundance, het bevechten van een eenvoudige wereld op de overvloed aan verschijnselen, Wijsgerig Perspectief (Uitgeverij Boom), 10 March 2008, as a corollary to the last book by Paul Feyerabemd, published posthumously with Terpstra as editor, Conquest of Abundance, A Tale of Abstraction versus the Richness of Being, University of Chicago Press, 1999.

(25) Stamboliev R., 1992, *The Energetics of Voice Dialogue, Facilitation in Transformational Psychology, An In-Depth Exploration of the Energetic Aspects of Transformational Psychology* 1992, LifeRhythm, P.O. Box 806, Mendocino CA 95460, ISBN 0-940795-12-9;

"In this book the energetic aspects of the psychological method of Voice Dialogue are explored, developed and demonstrated.

An overview of the consciousness model developed by Hal and Sidra Stone is presented as a foundation, to understand the energetic element in Voice Dialogue.

The book also utilizes selected material from the esoteric healing traditions and Tai Chi Ch'uan to give a larger understanding of basic principles operating in this facilitation technique. They enable movements and shifts of energy patterns in transformational work."

Definition of T'ai Chi Ch'uan (p. 81): "A Chinese martial art based on the principles of Taoism. Literally, the supreme, ultimate art of boxing. T'ai Chi Ch'uan is a method by which external affairs are regulated (self-defense) while the Chi (vital energy) is cultivated."

In connection with esoteric therapies:

Martina R., Van Walstijn P., 1999, Chi-neng, *Qi-Gong, Meditatie in beweging voor de westerse mens*, Andromeda, Blaricum, ISBN 90 5599 088 4.

Cohen K.S., 1997, *The Way of Qigong: The Art and Science of Chinese Energy Healing*, Ballantine Books, New York.

Von Rosenstiel I., 2009, *De kinderen van het Slotervaart* in het Parool's PS van de Week of Saturday 11 April 2009 (www.parool.nl), text and interview with Ines von Rosenstiel, paediatrician and head of the paediatrics department of the Slotervaartziekenhuis in Amsterdam, by Malika Sevil: "Only fifteen percent of the world population uses western medicine. The rest looks to traditional forms of medicine. For many chronic illness, the results are certainly not bad. This puts the arrogant idea that Western medicine is the only true form of medicine in an entirely different light."

Pop P., Van Dijk T., 2007, *Medische Missers, En hoe die voorkomen hadden kunnen worden* by Ton van Dijk, with commentary by Prof. P. Pop, Nijgh & Van Ditmar, Amsterdam, ISBN 978 90 388 9034 0: "Each year an estimated 1700 patients die in hospital because of medical errors, as appears from a recent report by the Dutch Association of Medical Specialists. Estimates of the number of deaths due to medical errors for the entire field of healthcare range from 5000 to 8000. In addition, every year around 30,000 people sustain unnecessary injuries due to errors during their treatment.
A revealing book on one of the biggest taboos in healthcare."

(26) Stone H., Winkelman S., 1985, *Embracing Our Selves*, De Vorss & Co., Marina Del Rey, CA.

On communication (p. 51; summary): "Voice Dialogue is in fact a method for communication."

This edition also refers to the Institute for Transformation Psychology (ITP) in Amsterdam (now in Bergen, the Netherlands) which is headed by Robert Stamboliev MA, Marian van Riemsdijk and Wieke Leenstra MSc and its Advisory Council, formed by Hal Stone PhD, Sidra Stone PhD, Jerien Koolbergen MSc and Prof. M.A.J. Romme. (www.voicedialogueworld.com and IVDA (International Voice Dialogue Agreement, International Voice Dialogue agreement on quality and ethics))

Stone H., Stone S., ibid., note (5).

In a word of thanks to this edition, Robert Stamboliev and Jerien Koolbergen are cited as the pioneers in the Netherlands because they "beautifully continued the work" of the authors and "have gathered around them a wonderful group of teachers and have contributed much to the further evolution of Voice Dialogue".

Vandereycken W., Van Deth R., 2003, Professor of Psychiatry at the University of Leuven and Ron van Deth, Psychologist, *Psychotherapie, Van theorie tot praktijk*, Bohn Stafleu Van Loghum, Houten/Antwerpen, ISBN 90 313 4166 5, p. 170 box 7-2: "Is alternative medicine really an alternative? ... alternative therapists often start from a holistic view of man: they regard human beings as a unity of body and mind. They emphasise, sometimes on the basis of spiritual constructs, the unique aspect of every human being and his or her possibilities to grow..... Voice Dialogue is akin to regular therapy ... [it helps] a person to become aware of his or her subpersonalities".

pp. 190-191, summary: "In practice, the choice of a treatment is sooner determined by the training and preference of the practitioner and the more or less coincidental availability of therapists in a region or institution..... Many therapists combine elements from several therapies (eclecticism, integration and synthesis)."

Mulder L., Budde J., 2008, *Drama in bedrijf, Werken met dramatechnieken in training en coaching*, Uitgeverij Thema, Zaltbommel, ISBN 978 90 5871 087 on Psycho-drama, Voice Dialogue, voice drama and other drama techniques.

(27) "Robert Stamboliev is an energy dancer and it is this sensitivity to energy that he has mastered and that he describes so well in this book. In a practical way he shows how the knowledge of, and sensitivity to the energetic process can be used quite directly in the practice of Voice Dialogue. He describes systematically the steps taken by the facilitator in preparing for and carrying out the work."

(28) Cf. the 'spiral of violence' mentioned by Achterhuis and the 'irrational violence' of Ger Groot.

Groot G., 2003, *Vier ongemakkelijke filosofen, Nietzsche, Cioran, Bataille, Derrida*, Uitgeverij SUN, Amsterdam, ISBN 90 5875 016 7.

Achterhuis defines 'irrational violence' as "the endless struggle of forces concealed behind the humanist Western Enlightenment culture ... the evil and violence that have been excluded from our culture".

It is interesting to see how Hans Achterhuis and Ger Groot think that the problems in this area should be dealt with.

Achterhuis on Ger Groot: "In the end he largely distances himself from it. It is undoubtedly thanks to their insights (from Nietzsche to Derrida, author) that we have become aware of the precarious and unstable balance 'of reasonableness, justice, prudence and moderation, that European culture aims to be' (Groot 2003, p. 503). But Groot refuses to follow the philosophers he discusses and make a frontal attack on this unstable structure as they do."

Achterhuis tentatively agrees: "It is true of both persons and cultures that, if they acknowledge their dark sides, and perhaps know how to handle them best, *they will ultimately take their distance from them* (emphasis added by author). In her large-scale study of religious terrorism, Jessica Stern goes one step further. Invoking Jung, who saw evil as an archetypical shadow in every person, she thinks that this shadow can be integrated in our actions, even leading to creativity (Stern 2005, p. 20). Such a conclusion seems to me to be too quick and easy. Groot's position remains my starting point as well."

In this context I opt for the solution put forward by Voice Dialogue (the psychology of the selves, primary and disowned selves) of Hal and Sidra Stone (Dialogues 5), which greatly resembles Stern's approach. However, in the former the process of consciousness is primary: it can be used to make deliberate choices while giving careful consideration to all interests, or in the terms of Voice Dialogue, to all subpersonalities or energy patterns. This makes it clear that violence is not inherent in human nature, but that people can make choices in this respect and take responsibility for them.

(29) Rosenberg M.B., 2003, *Non-violent Communication: A Language of Compassion*, Puddledancer Press, ISBN-10: 1892005034 and ISBN-13: 978-1892005038.

(30) Lamme V.A.F., 2009, interview by Manon Sikkel in Spui Gesprek, 29 - 2009/1 (April 2009) [*Bewustzijn: het geheim van het brein*].

Lamme V.A.F., 2010, *De vrije wil bestaat niet, Over wie er echt de baas is in het brein*, Uitgeverij Bert Bakker, Amsterdam, ISBN 978 90 351 3539 0.

(31) Lamme V.A.F., 2006, Trends in Cognitive Sciences 10, 494-501 (2006), *Towards a True Neural Stance on Consciousness*.

(32) Habermas J., Ratzinger J., 2005, *Dialektik der Säkularisierung. Über Vernunft und Religion*, Libreria Editrice Vaticana; Verlag Herder, Freiburg im Breisgau; Edizioni San Paolo s.r.l.; English translation: *The Dialectics of Secularization, On Reason and Religion*, Ignatius Press, San Francisco, CA 94118, 2008, ISBN 978 158 617 1667.

(33) Bakker R., 1984, philosopher, theologian and classicist, emeritus professor, Central Interfaculty of Groningen University in *Studia in honorem Reinout Bakker*, presented by the Centrale Interfaculteit Rijksuniversiteit Groningen, ed. B. Delfgaauw, H. Hubbeling, W. Smith:

"Can philosophical anthropology still exist?

... philosophical anthropology is a domain unto itself, and cannot be replaced by any other anthropology. The final explanation of man lies **outside** all possible scientific views that have ever been formulated, because they lie within the origins of every branch of science, including the science of philosophy. It is the final ground on which the philosophies, of any nature whatsoever, can be practised implicitly or explicitly.

... In my inaugural speech of 25 January 1965 I spoke of the necessary collaboration between philosophy and science. Philosophy without contact with the empirical sciences is empty, but also: the empirical sciences are blind without the contribution of philosophy. If one of these two poles is made absolute, the danger of gross onesidedness, or even distortion, is imminent.

The fact that the ultimate questions about man are so rarely asked stems from giving the scientific foundation of philosophy an absolute status. Many phenomenologists and existentialists have warned against such scientism.
... The methods of a post-modern philosophical anthropology will have to be based on reflection, on the claim that it is possible to debate differences and contrasts on reasonable grounds, and on the individual responsibility for the decisions we all make for ourselves in respect of changes in body and mind. A post-modern version of Sartre's creed: man is and always will be what he makes of himself."

It contains the following references:

Bakker R., 1982, *Wijsgerige antropologie van de twintigste eeuw*, Assen, 1982, 3; Cf. J. van Praag, *Levensovertuiging, filosofie en wetenschap*, 1979 and R. Bakker, *Noodzakelijke samenwerking, Merleau-Ponty's bijdrage tot het gesprek tussen filosofie en wetenschap*, Groningen, 1965.

See also Dr. M.F. Fresco, endowed chair, Centrale Interfaculteit Rijksuniversiteit Leiden in Levensberichten, *Reinout Bakker, Minnertsga, the Netherlands, 2 November 1920 - Spain 25 March 1987.*

Two more references:

Bakker R., 1987, *Filosofie en wetenschap*, Kampen 1987. (Reprint of Bakker's inaugural speech and his farewell lecture, published and with an introduction by B. Delfgaauw.)

Bakker R., 1986, (A reprint has also been published of Merleau-Ponty, *Voorwoord tot de fenomenologie van de waarneming. Ingeleid, vertaald en geannoteerd door dr. R. Bakker*, Kampen 1986)

(34) Shouldn't we start examining the words 'religiosity' and 'religion' in advance before trying to prove the existence of God, because what is behind those words first of all could be considered as a human emotion, namely the deepest desire for unity (breaking out of isolation) and secondly as a mystery, to be defined by every culture in its own way (relevance: diverse and equal), so that we can perhaps build a bridge between the world's religions?

Religiosity (in a broad sense, spirituality, mysticism, etc.) of human beings as absolute entities is a matter that takes place on the playing field of the illusion and should therefore be regarded as strictly personal. If people turn their religious feelings into a religion (in a narrow sense), then we may speak of permanence in their communication, set down in books, in which its evolution and history and meaning are described, thus providing it with a certain legitimacy as a religion. Some religions go even further in this respect by creating a wide range of societal institutions such as churches and organisations that provide social services (in a broad sense), so as to anchor themselves in society.

Smart N., 2011, The World's Religions, ISBN 978-0-521-63748-0

(35) NRC Handelsblad Friday 22 June 2007 (www.nrc.nl), Cultureel Supplement, Filosofie Beschouwing.

(36) *Encyclopedie van de Filosofie*, ibid., note (12):

"*Humanism in contemporary philosophy*

In contemporary philosophy, humanism tends more to make itself a subject of debate rather than a defined school of thought with a fixed programme. Humanists want to openly relate to the critics of the classical humanist picture of man, which consists in autonomy, self-determination and atheism, and to seek a more qualified definition of humanism. This attitude often acts as a bridge between humanism on the one hand and religious feelings and spirituality on the other, and the significance of humanism is then not so much a clearly delineated life philosophy as it is a creative, practical social-political movement to search for meaning, to humanise society and culture and to discover new forms of the art of living.

Organised humanism maintains its position in the Netherlands as an academic and social addition to the traditional social pillars, coming to expression in the Humanist Alliance, founded in 2001.

Attempts are also being made in Islamic philosophy to develop a humanism that builds on the age-old humanist traditions in Islam and is strongly anti-fundamentalist. Arkoun was an important spokesperson for this, as was Nas'r Abu Zayd (1943-), a humanist scholar who worked in the Netherlands.

Duyndam J., Poorthuis M., De Wit Th.W.A., 2005, (red.), *Humanisme en religie. Controverses, bruggen, perspectieven*.

Kunneman H., 2005, *Voorbij het dikke-ik. Bouwstenen voor een kritisch humanisme*".

(37) Tallon A., Williams P., 1982, Memorial Minutes James Joseph Dagenais 1923-1981, *Proceedings and Addresses of the American Philosophical Association*, Vol. 56, No. 2, (Nov., 1982), pp. 253-255, Published by American Philosophical Association, Stable URL: http://www.jstor.org/stable/3131239:

"James J. Dagenais was born in Blue Island, Illinois, in 1923, attended St. Ignatius High School in Chicago, and upon graduation entered the Society of Jesus to begin the fifteen years of spiritual exercises, academic studies, and practical training geared toward production of that enigmatic figure, shrouded in legend (to believe Rene Fulop-Miller) of power and secrecy – the Jesuit. Among his early academic achievements: an M.A. in philosophy from Loyola University (Chicago), with a thesis on "Kierkegaard and Belief"; a Licentiate in Theology from West Baden College (Indiana), with a study on "Some Christou in Pauline Texts". Next came a break from the studies as he moved to the other side of the desk to teach for several years at the University of Detroit High School, after which Jim went to Louvain University (Leuven, Belgium). At the Institut Supérieur de Philosophie Jim entered fully into the best continental program of graduate philosophical studies available, becoming a committed member of the phenomenological movement, while also taking advantage of Louvain's proximity to Paris, where at Nanterre and the Sorbonne there was available a full-spirited complement to the Belgian approach, with its many and thorough courses; in particular Jim spent a considerable amount of time studying with Paul Ricoeur. In 1966, having completed his Docteur en Philosophie - his dissertation was a phenomenological critique of the work of Carl Rogers - he accepted appointment to the Department of Religion at Miami University (Oxford, Ohio).

At Miami Jim's life took a major turn as he left the Jesuits soon after arriving at Oxford and married Francoise Monnoyer de Galland. Francoise, a native of Belgium, a psychologist, and a person whose instant presence, quiet cultivation, and deep spirituality immediately and permanently impress all who meet her, shared Jim's broad academic interests and political involvements. We all can remember what those mid and late sixties were like nationally. At Miami Jim was especially concerned in that troubled era to promote communication between the increasingly polarized faction in the Oxford community and publicly expressed his dismay over the breakdown of mutual understanding which his own school of philosophy sought to promote. He attempted more than once to serve as a bridge-builder, as in team-teaching "Dimensions of Dialogue" at Miami and in his initiative in convening the "Conference on the Epistemological Relationships between Sciences and the Humanities" at Miami in 1975 and 1976, a series of meetings still exerting influence far beyond the Miami campus."

(38) Dagenais J.J., 1972, *Models of Man, A Phenomenological Critique of Some Paradigms in the Human Sciences*, Martinus Nijhoff/The Hague, ISBN 90 247 1290 4.

(39) Van Praag J.P., 1965, *Wat is humanistiek*? Rede, uitgesproken bij de aanvaarding van het ambt van bijzonder hoogleraar vanwege de humanistische Stichting Socrates in de humanistiek en de antropologie van het humanisme bij de Rijksuniversiteit Leiden, 21 mei 1965 [Inaugural speech, 21 May 1965] (www.human.nl).

(40) *Encyclopedie van de Filosofie*, ibid., noot (12):

"In *humanistic* studies, a new multidisciplinary scientific school of thought linking philosophy, religious studies, theory of philosophy of life, ethics, social sciences, critical organisational studies and practical subjects, new meanings of humanism are being explored and tested."

(41) Gasenbeek B., Brabers J., Kuijlman W., 2006, *Een huis voor humanisten: het Humanistisch Verbond (1946-2006)*; the intentions and draft policy plans expressed are fully in line with this (www.human.nl).

(42) Van Praag J.P., 1979, *Levensovertuiging, filosofie en wetenschap*, Farewell lecture at Leiden University, 13 November 1979 (www.human.nl).

(43) Roessler B., 2005, *Humanisme en Religie, Tijdschrift voor Humanistiek*, Vol. 6, No. 24, December 2005: "Should a humanism that is open to criticism really have a religious dimension, an inexplicable rest that forms the foundation of our existence? In my opinion, no." (www.human.nl).

(44) Russell B., (United Kingdom 1872-1970) in *Encyclopedie van de Filosofie*, ibid., note (12):

"*Methodological and epistemological standpoints*

Russell defended a methodical principle for philosophy that is known as Ockham's razor: 'Do not expand the number of entities assumed to exist any further than strictly necessary.' For Russell, this principle embodied a programme for general philosophical analysis: 'If possible, replace entities which we think exist (such as physical objects, the human ego) by logical constructs made up of entities which we are sure exist.' These logical constructs are immediate observations (cf. Chapter VIII, J.J. Dagenais's 'experiencing before any kind of conscious thematization' in his definition of philosophical anthropology and Chapter XIII Core Concepts; author), set forth in basic statements such as 'This x is red', 'This is next to that', and so on. Russell was primarily interested in how we can have knowledge of the external world. He tried to answer this question by showing how we can construct complex insights from basic statements about that world."

(45) In his foreword to *De vrije wil bestaat niet* this picture is emphatically confirmed, first of all in the way in which this title was suggested to him by his publisher, who "made it up on the spot", which he "had a hard time getting used to [at first], but quickly saw that this title would be a good umbrella which would allow the book to include much more than just the unconscious".

He explicitly renounced philosophy, stating that "discussions about free will often degenerate into metaphysical-philosophical claptrap about determinism ... which neither adds much to nor subtracts much from our sense of free will." (Cf. Susan Blackmore on this in notes (5) and (13)).

He winds up by stressing the fact that his book primarily deals with "the influences exerted on the brain as we carry out behaviour and take decisions" in relation to a number of topics that are in fact derived from philosophy, which he refers to as "rationalism and deliberation", "thoughts - in the form of language or otherwise", "a controlling 'ego' that uses thoughts and logic to determine our choices". So Lamme does not restrict himself to his own domain of cognitive neuroscience, but also enters the domain of philosophical anthropology without expressing himself further on it.

(46) Prof. Dr. Cheung Chan Fai
B.A., M.Phil. (CUHK), Dr. phil. (Freiburg)

Office of University General Education
The Chinese University of Hong Kong

Room 803, Hui Yeung Shing Building,
The Chinese University of Hong Kong

Tel: (852)2609 7075/2609 7563
Fax: (852)2603 5398
Email: oge@cuhk.edu.hk
Website: www.cuhk.edu.hk/oge

Director of University General Education,
Professor and Chairman, Department of Philosophy,

Director, Edwin Cheng Foundation Asian Centre for Phenomenology,
Director, Research Centre for General Education,
Director, Leadership Development Programme,
The Chinese University of Hong Kong

Research Interests

Phenomenology, esp. Husserl and Heidegger philosophy
History of Western philosophy
Philosophy of love
Philosophy of death
Utopian thought
Philosophy of happiness

Tel: 2609 7138
Fax: 2603 5323
Email: cheungcf@cuhk.edu.hk

(47) Cheung Chan Fai, 2001, Human Nature and Human Existence
- On the Problem of the Distinction Between Man and Animal,
收《天人之　際與人禽之辨—比較與多元的觀點》，《新亞學術集刊》，第十七期（2001），頁365–383。

(48) Descartes R., 2006, Over de methode, Boom Klassiek, ISBN 90 5352 791 5

(49) Kant I., 1800, Anthropologie
Kant I, 2004, Kritiek van de Zuivere Rede, Boom, ISBN 90 5352 702 8
Kant I, 1999, Prolegomena, Uitgeverij Boom, Amsterdam, ISBN 90 5352 318 9

(50) Heidegger M, 1947, Brief über den Humanismus.

(51) Van Praag J.P., 1994, The Foundations Of Humanism, Prometheus Books, ISBN 10: 087975163 and ISBN 13: 9780879751678

(52) Landmann M., 1979, Philosophische Anthropologie, Menschliche Selbstdeutung in Geschichte und Gegenwart, Walter de Gruyter & Co., Berlin (1964,1955)

(53) UNESCO e-magazine for culture and philosophy Philosophical Views, ISSUE 4, 2017, pp.35-36

(54) This essay has been published in the Journal of Philosophical Investigations of the University of Tabriz (Iran), Volume 12, Issue 24, Article 10/11, Autumn 2018, pp. 201-218 and has also been accepted for the International Conference on New Frontiers in Engineering, Sience, Law, Management, Humanities and Social Science 2019, INFES-2019, to be held at IST-GAUHATI UNIVERSITY, GUWAHATI, INDIA between 23-24 February 2019.

XIII Core concepts

Essential (Relative Freedom)

The origin and evolution* of human beings as absolute entities can be divided into five distinctive segments:

1 Cosmos, which cannot be defined, but which has the following characteristics: Intelligence (Plan, Order, Structure), Energy, Form and Matter
2 Planet Earth and Nature (Laws of Nature)
3 Human Beings: Brain, Male and Female, Reproductive Urge
4 Conception (Insemination), Duality, Birth
5 Unity, Absolute Entity

The defining essential characteristics* of human beings as absolute entities are:

1 Dependency and Urge for Survival (Material)
2 Inward-looking (Closed), Goal in Itself (Autonomy, Being Yourself), Isolation and Communication (Broad, Immaterial)
3 Identity (Singularity, Character) and Individuality
4 Ultimate Objective: Self-Fulfilment (Development, Search for Meaning)
5 Autonomy (Self-Determination) and Freedom (Relative Freedom)

As absolute entities, human beings operate by means of experience*. Experience as a concept can be described as parts, or phases, of processes in the brain. These processes are autonomous. Accordingly, experience can be divided into the following parts or phases:

1 Observation (Input)
2 Storage (Memory)
3 Organising (Combining)
4 Conclusion or Finding (Mood, Intuition, Feelings, Emotions, Thought, Knowledge, Reason, Idea, Mental Grasp, Consciousness, Mind, Soul, Psyche, Will, Conscience, etc.)
5 Plan
6 Performance (Output)

Relational (Absolute Freedom)

Communication*

In simple terms, communication is an attempt to connect (make an imaginary connection) with another human being. Clearly, however, a great deal can go wrong, resulting in miscommunication or misunderstandings. In everyday dealings this takes place (incidentally, fleetingly) in our direct contacts with other persons, against a background of economic or simply social reasons (exchange of information (in a broad sense), networking). In relation to the second essential characteristic of human beings as absolute entities, this refers to the communication for other reasons, and it can therefore take place in all other fields in which people are active. Typical of this type of communication is that the content of the message is considerably more complex; direct contact is inadequate for its transfer, so that some other means (indirect, with a permanent form) must be sought, thus giving communication a permanence in our lives. Texts, textbooks, image and sound recordings are permanent forms of communication. Religion and philosophy, art and culture, science and politics are expressions of this and therefore also belong to the world of the imagination.

We must also make a distinction between forms of communication (the means) and the content of the message they put across. As we have seen, communication entails a fair chance of misunderstanding or miscommunication. This means that, to actually put a message across, the sender must have a clear idea of its contents. The sender must correctly translate the contents of the message into the means of communication of choice, so that the recipient of the message can reasonably be expected to understand it (in an objective sense). The recipient will receive the message via his or her own process of experience, thus colouring the translation, which is now different from the original intention of the sender. The original intention of the sender can be approached more closely by conducting further or more intensive communication until both sender and recipient have the impression that the communication properly reflects the intention.

Means of communication are thus expressions of what people experience, of the process of experience that they perceive and of which they are part, that they are themselves. They manifest themselves outside people's introversion in a sort of space that we could term the playing field of illusion, where the exchange takes place, by which the link is made.

Power*

When a person exercises power in a way that is contrary to the interests or against the will of others, it makes a caricature of that person's power or the person exercising it. Such exercise of power is contrary to the nature of human beings as absolute entities and therefore contrary to their being and their essential characteristics.

Specifically, being in a position of power and wielding power have an effect on our relationships with other people, one in which there is a role for morals and ethics. It is always a matter between individuals, each of whom work in their own way to promote their own interests. But when they are unable to promote certain of their interests on their own, they will band together, something that takes place in all fields imaginable. When they take this step, human beings as absolute entities step outside of themselves, thus shaping a form of co-existence the nature of which can be both material and immaterial: immaterial because they are driven together by a shared motive, and material when, as a group, they give shape to their collaboration by setting up a range of social institutions. This manner of promoting individual and collective interests knows no bounds, and will always result in the unlimited pursuit of their own interests and the related unbridled exercise of power, which inevitably leads to all manner of social problems. Moreover, it implies an incessant struggle (between individuals) and war (between groups), things people commonly engage in yet today.

The democratic rule of law*

People only recently came to understand this, and they developed the concept of a democratic constitutional state, which created a basis for living together peacefully. The chief characteristic of a constitutional democracy is that people subject themselves to its regime voluntarily, thus legitimating the power it holds as well as its exercise. But there are limits to anything to which people voluntarily subject themselves, and the objectives of a constitutional democracy must largely be in line with promotion of the individual and collective interests of its subjects, on whose support the constitutional democracy must be able to rely. These are primarily economic interests (aimed at survival).

Democracy can thus exert its influence on society as a whole as well as on the individual citizens, and the longer its period of development (the higher the degree of organisation it has attained), the more will its influence be felt. The immaterial concept of the constitutional democracy has taken shape in the form of material democratic institutions that are anchored in society. Thanks to the present high organisational level of most Western democracies, nearly all societal institutions are amply legitimated and derive their identity from this, allowing them to share some of the state's power and endowing them with certain competencies or powers to act to the exclusion of others (they enjoy exclusivity). Despite the fact that citizens and societal institutions enjoy a large degree of freedom to act as they see fit, government has gained a considerable grip on society as a whole. As a result, it has been able to set limits to competition and rivalry and to power and its exercise (cartels, monopolies, etc.) by means of legislation, and to enforce compliance, if necessary with the use of violence.

Beyond the scope of economic life, and especially on the playing field of illusion (permanent forms of communication), government influence should be kept to a minimum because this is the exclusive domain of individual citizens. It should be reserved to them because it is where they can bring to expression their essential characteristics as absolute entities (communication, identity, the search for meaning, autonomy), areas in which they ought to be entirely free. These essential characteristics have therefore acquired an important place within a constitutional democracy in the form of basic rights and freedoms that protect citizens against the power of the state (freedom of opinion, of association and meeting, mental and physical integrity, religion etc.). In fact the role of the government can largely be defined as creating the frameworks in which individual citizens can move freely (or as freely as possible).

Conscience (morals and ethics)*

Conscience is respect for the interests of others; it is based on self-respect, which may lead you to decide to subject your dealings with other people to a set of standards for yourself and try to encourage others to do the same. From this point of view, good means good for yourself and therefore for others as well. You realise that when you injure another person, you primarily harm yourself. Here we enter the area of morals and ethics, to which we can attach a complete moral philosophy and on the basis of a faith, a moral theology. At the end of this road is total love of yourself and others, because you have come to realise that it is the only way that can lead to the fourth essential characteristic of people as absolute entities, namely self-fulfilment. You will then have developed in a way that allows you to give yourself and others scope that we need as absolute entities (compassion, solidarity).

XIV About the author

"Every day, eight billion people are all trying to find their own way. Only two aspects are important here: the way in which each of them does this individually, and their mutual relations", according to author Hans Dassen (Eindhoven, the Netherlands, 1944). The path taken by Dassen's own life served as the source of inspiration for this new philosophy of man. Before setting out on a full theoretical description of this philosophy, Dassen introduces us to it in a practical sense: dialogues with a writer, contemporary philosophers, psychologists and the Pope.

Dassen's path has been a colourful succession of experiences both professional and private. In the 1970s and 1980s he was a successful lawyer and solicitor in The Hague; he advised the Christian Democratic group in the Dutch Lower House on social issues and served as a consultant to and officer of a number of bodies represented in the Social and Economic Council of the Netherlands. In his work, he repeatedly found himself confronted with issues in relation to truth and wisdom, in which he developed a deep interest. Parallel to his professional development, Dassen was always greatly interested in painting, mainly by French artists. The art of painting - modern painting in particular - elicited questions about beauty and convinced him to become an amateur philosopher. Resolved to further his development in the field of philosophy and ethics, he undertook course work at the University of Amsterdam. This book, on a new philosophy of man, is the result not only of his personal search but more importantly, the answers he found.

In addition to this book setting forth his philosophy, Dassen publishes articles, while his ideas can be found on Anthroopos.com. This website is part of Dassen's Anthroopos foundation which he established in 2008 to stimulate further scientific research, dialogue and public debate on philosophical anthropology.

Dassen also pioneers as a philosophy coach. Based on his own philosophy, he and his clients examine how ethical, social or political issues can have an inhibiting or liberating effect on personal or business choice processes. Dassen has two adult sons and lives in Amsterdam together with his partner.

Since 9 December 2016 Dassen is a member of the Advisory and Editorial Board, as well as National Delegate of the Netherlands of the UNESCO e-magazine for culture and philosophy "Filozofski pogledi/Philosophical Views" (ISSN 2466-3514 (online) & Thomson Reuters RID: Q-2899-2016) from Belgrade.

Berg en Terblijt, July 2022

XV Dedicated to

Prof. Dr. Reinout Bakker

Minnertsga, the Netherlands, 2 November 1920 - Spain, 25 March 1987
Philosopher, theologian and classicist
Emeritus professor, Groningen University

When, in his farewell speech in 1984, he asked himself despairingly, "Can philosophical anthropology still exist?", the wish was father to the thought.
During his tenure in Groningen (1965 - 1984) he had cleared the way for this by passionately dedicating himself to Phenomenology of Perception by Maurice Merleau-Ponty (France 1908 - 1961) and existentialism while underpinning this by devoting well-earned attention to his disowned side in Michel Foucault's (France 1926 - 1984) structuralism, with a view to toning it down; it was his belief that philosophical anthropology revolves around individuals, and people can never be set down in structures. "A philosophy that does not want its subject to be bound by structures must take structuralism seriously."

I have tried to build on this by portraying individual human beings as absolute entities that emerge from the process of experience, growing awareness and consciousness-raising in which they are involved. It is my sincere hope that this has demonstrated that, in the 21st century, Reinout Bakker's question can finally be answered in the affirmative.

A heartfelt wish of Reinout Bakker's would have been fulfilled if he had known that in the 2009-2010 school year a philosophy symposium would be held, devoted to the theme of that year's final exam in philosophy: it had been made an elective subject in secondary schools. He was of the opinion that philosophy cannot be taught early enough and often enough, and much of his life was spent securing a place in the school curriculum for this subject.